MONOGRAPHS OF THE
SOCIETY FOR RESEARCH IN
CHILD DEVELOPMENT

Serial No. 251, Vol. 62, No. 3, 1997

LEARNING IN THE DEVELOPMENT
OF INFANT LOCOMOTION

Karen E. Adolph

WITH COMMENTARY BY

Bennett I. Bertenthal
Steven M. Boker
Eugene C. Goldfield
Eleanor J. Gibson

MONOGRAPHS OF THE SOCIETY FOR RESEARCH IN CHILD DEVELOPMENT
Serial No. 251, Vol. 62, No. 3, 1997

CONTENTS

ABSTRACT

ADOLPH, KAREN E. Learning in the Development of Infant Locomotion. With Commentary by BENNETT I. BERTENTHAL and STEVEN M. BOKER, by EUGENE C. GOLDFIELD, and by ELEANOR J. GIBSON. *Monographs of the Society for Research in Child Development*, 1997, **62**(3, Serial No. 251).

Infants master crawling and walking in an environment filled with varied and unfamiliar surfaces. At the same time, infants' bodies and skills continually change. The changing demands of everyday locomotion require infants to adapt locomotion to the properties of the terrain and to their own physical abilities. This *Monograph* examines how infants acquire adaptive locomotion in a novel task—going up and down slopes. Infants were tested longitudinally from their first week of crawling until several weeks after they began walking.

Everyday locomotor experience played a central role in adaptive responding. Over weeks of crawling, infants' judgments became increasingly accurate, and exploration became increasingly efficient. There was no transfer over the transition from crawling to walking. Instead, infants learned, all over again, how to cope with slopes from an upright position. Findings indicate that learning generalized from everyday experience traveling over flat surfaces at home but that learning was specific to infants' typical method of locomotion and vantage point. Moreover, learning was not the result of simple associations between a particular locomotor response and a particular slope. Rather, infants learned to gauge their abilities on-line as they encountered each hill at the start of the trial. Change in locomotor responses and exploratory movements revealed a process of differentiation and selection spurred by changes in infants' everyday experience, body dimensions, and locomotor proficiency on flat ground.

I. RELEVANCE OF INFANT LOCOMOTION FOR UNDERSTANDING DEVELOPMENT

This *Monograph* presents a new view of locomotor development—the processes involved in acquiring adaptive mobility. Previous research on infant locomotion has focused on the ages and stages of locomotor milestones or on biomechanical changes in proficiency of infants' gait. Researchers know surprisingly little, however, about how infants acquire the wherewithal to navigate the everyday environment. Infants do not achieve mobility on the white pages of a textbook milestone chart or on the homogeneous surface of a typical laboratory floor. Rather, infants master the biomechanics of crawling and walking in an environment filled with varied surfaces, obstacles, paths, and places. All the while, infants' bodies and skills are continually changing.

The present study was designed to redress limitations of previous research. The *Monograph* reports a longitudinal investigation of infants' ability to adapt movements to variations in the terrain and to changes in their physical capabilities. The aims were to further our understanding of the processes involved in adaptive locomotion and to present a clearer picture of how experience, age, growth, and skill contribute to developmental change.

TRADITIONAL RESEARCH ON INFANT LOCOMOTION

Fifty years ago, the study of infant locomotion was a boomtown of activity. Spurred by the promise of relating change in motor abilities to maturation of neural structures, pioneering researchers in the 1930s and 1940s filled textbooks, scientific journals, and parent guides with extensive catalogs of the remarkable parade of skills en route to independent mobility (e.g., Burnside, 1927; McGraw, 1945; Shirley, 1931). Gesell and his colleagues, for example, identified 22 stages in the development of crawling, beginning when infants first lift their heads from a prone position, proceeding through diffuse movements of arms and legs during belly crawling, and ending when babies crawl firmly across the floor on their hands and knees (e.g., Gesell & Ames, 1940;

1

Gesell & Thompson, 1938). McGraw (1945) described seven primary stages in the development of walking, progressing from newborns' reflexive stepping movements to the inhibition of alternating leg movements in early infancy and finally culminating in independent walking at the end of the first year. Inferences about the neurological underpinnings of locomotor milestones figured prominently in early editions of the Carmichael *Handbook* (e.g., Gesell, 1946, 1954; McGraw, 1946).

Ironically, the widespread acceptance of neuromuscular maturation as the primary mechanism of developmental change brought further research to a standstill (Goldfield, 1989; Thelen, 1995; Thelen & Adolph, 1992). Once psychologists had established the normal trajectory of locomotor development and identified brain maturation as the primary cause of developmental change, there seemed little else to learn. From the 1950s to the 1980s, research on infant locomotion was a virtual ghost town in psychological circles. Chapters on motor development were conspicuously absent from the Mussen *Handbook* and psychological publications. Research on development of locomotion was restricted largely to clinical and cross-cultural comparisons (e.g., Konner, 1976; Super, 1976) or to descriptive studies of children's gait in medical or biomechanics tracts (e.g., Bernstein, 1967; Burnett & Johnson, 1971; Grieve & Gear, 1966; Sutherland, Olshen, Cooper, & Woo, 1980).

RECENT SYSTEMS APPROACHES TO INFANT LOCOMOTION

In the 1980s, new systems approaches to motor development stimulated a resurgence of interest in infant locomotion (Pick, 1989; Thelen, 1989). In particular, sophisticated, new technologies for recording rapid movements in infants facilitated more finely grained, quantitative analyses of biomechanical changes in locomotor movements (e.g., Bril & Breniere, 1989, 1991; Clark & Phillips, 1987; Freedland & Bertenthal, 1994; Shumway-Cook & Woollacott, 1985; Thelen & Ulrich, 1991). Modern researchers use high-speed film, computerized video recordings, automatic digitizing of anatomical landmarks, infrared-emitting diodes, surface EMG, and force plates to observe moment-to-moment changes in proficiency of kicking, crawling, upright stance, and walking. Information about interlimb phasing, joint angles, muscle firing, and so on has led to a deeper understanding of change in coordination, balance, and strength as infants' gait becomes more skillful and proficient.

More important, the methodological innovations and conceptual advances of the new systems approaches point to general principles for understanding developmental change (e.g., Gibson, 1994a, 1994b; Smith & Thelen, 1993). In particular, research on infant locomotion provides fresh insights into the origin of new behaviors and the conundrum of reconciling underlying continuity with stage-like discontinuities in children's performance

(Thelen & Smith, 1994). For example, maturation of neural structures was the classic explanation for the origin of independent walking and the stage-like appearance, disappearance, and subsequent reappearance of alternating "walking" movements over infants' first year of life (McGraw, 1940, 1945, 1946). According to this explanation, myelination of the corticospinal tract inhibits newborns' reflexive stepping, and later intentional walking awaits sufficient maturation for cortical control.

Recent research, however, indicates that continuity of walking movements throughout the first year may be masked by underlying changes in the relative distribution of infants' muscle mass and body fat, ongoing improvements in postural control, and the differential effects of gravity (Thelen, 1986; Thelen & Fisher, 1982; Thelen, Fisher, & Ridley-Johnson, 1984; Thelen & Ulrich, 1991). Newborns with chubbier legs stepped less than more slender-legged infants. When slim legs were weighted with the amount of fat typically gained over the first few months of life, infants stopped stepping. When the pull of gravity was mitigated by placing chubby infants on their backs or submerging them waist deep in a tank of water, babies exhibited alternating leg movements. Likewise, when leg strength and balance control were bolstered by supporting infants upright over a motorized treadmill, babies stepped. When the same infants were required to generate all the muscle forces for lifting their legs in an upright position or were expected to keep their balance in independent walking, they stood rooted to the ground or toppled over.

These findings from infant leg movements suggest that continuous, ongoing changes in underlying constituents can produce new behavioral patterns and engender stage-like discontinuities in development (Thelen & Smith, 1994). In this case, some constituents of change are in infants' brains, some in the rest of their bodies, and some in the task constraints. At various points in development, the key to change may reside in the most psychologically interesting structures or in the most peripheral and innocuous elements of the system.

LEARNING FROM LOCOMOTOR EXPERIENCE

Infant locomotion provides a unique window into understanding processes of change because independent mobility invites new opportunities for learning. Mobile infants can learn about the larger layout and about their own capabilities relative to new worlds of surfaces and places (Gibson, 1988; Gibson & Schmuckler, 1989; Piaget, 1954). After infants begin to crawl, they can go see what is behind a barrier or around the corner. They can view landmarks from changing perspectives and learn about places and paths between locales. For the first time, infants can initiate exploration away from caregivers (Gustafson, 1984; Martinsen, 1982) and establish new independence of thought and action (Biringen, Emde, Campos, & Appelbaum, 1995; Mahler, Pine, & Bergman, 1975). When infants stand up and begin to walk, they have an expanded outlook over the terrain ahead; they can peer over the edges of things with more of a bird's-eye view. Toddlers' hands are freed from supporting their bodies, and they can carry objects from place to place.

Empirical studies suggest that infants may use information obtained during locomotion to facilitate improvements in a variety of laboratory tasks (e.g., Acredolo, 1988; Bertenthal & Campos, 1990; Campos & Bertenthal, 1984). For example, seeing and feeling themselves walk around is critical for visually guided reaching, placing, and avoidance responses in kittens (Hein & Diamond, 1972; Held & Hein, 1963). In human infants, crawling experience is related to infants' ability to negotiate detours (Lockman, 1984) and to increased use of environmental landmarks to mark the location of interesting events or hidden objects (e.g., Acredolo, Adams, & Goodwyn, 1984; Bai & Bertenthal, 1992; Benson & Uzgiris, 1985; Kermoian & Campos, 1988).

More central to this *Monograph*, recent research suggests that adaptive locomotion may itself require learning. The step-to-step demands of everyday mobility create new challenges for adaptive responding. Infants' homes contain a variety of floor coverings, paths cluttered with furniture and obstacles, and stairs leading from one area to the next; outdoor play yards may be flat, sloping, spongy, rigid, slippery, rough, and so on. All the while, babies must adapt newfound methods of locomotion to the changing postural constraints of their growing bodies. Changeable task constraints mean that adaptive mobility requires a continual, on-line decision-making process about how to navigate the ground ahead safely. Infants must decide how to go down stairs or how to traverse a slippery linoleum floor. They must decide whether the glass coffee table provides adequate support for their weight or whether climbing out of the crib is a wise idea.

As described in the following chapter, recent research suggests that infants may learn adaptive control of locomotor movements from everyday experience coping with balance requirements as they travel around their homes and play yards. For example, duration of crawling experience is related to avoidance and accelerated heart rate on a visual cliff (e.g., Campos, Bertenthal, & Kermoian, 1992). Walking experience is related to visual control of balance in upright stance (Stoffregen, Schmuckler, & Gibson, 1987) and appropriate locomotor responses on safe versus risky slopes (Adolph, 1995).

Despite suggestive evidence linking locomotor experience to adaptive behavior in laboratory tasks, we still know very little about the causes of infants' accomplishments and blunders as they pit their new locomotor capabilities against the changing demands of the everyday environment. There has been surprisingly little progress made toward describing what infants might learn via everyday experience or the nature of the learning process. Furthermore, locomotor experience is correlated with infants' age and age-related changes in infants' bodies and skills, but researchers know little about the relative contributions of age, experience, growth, and skill factors. As described below, most research to date has provided static snapshots of infants' performance at particular ages or particular points before or after they become mobile, with little attention to how locomotion becomes flexibly organized and adapted to dynamically changing tasks.

A first step toward understanding adaptive locomotion is a description of the task constraints and potential sources of information. The following chapter reviews previous research on infants' ability to adapt to variations in the terrain.

II. ADAPTIVE LOCOMOTION:
SOURCES OF INFORMATION AND TASK CONSTRAINTS

Adaptive locomotion depends on the match between animals' current capabilities and the properties of the supporting surface—what Gibson (1979) termed *affordances*. The surface must provide a continuous path to support the body, must be large enough to allow passage as the body moves forward, must be sturdy enough to support body weight, and must be firm enough, be flat enough, and have sufficient friction to maintain balance as weight shifts from limb to limb (Adolph, Eppler, & Gibson, 1993b; Stoffregen & Riccio, 1988).

Everyday locomotion involves a continual, on-line decision-making process because the terrain is unpredictable and animals' physical capabilities are changeable. Variations in local conditions require continuous modification of ongoing movements, such as when we turn to fit through a revolving door or shorten step length to navigate a tricky patch of ice. Changes in physical capabilities necessitate selection from among a variety of locomotor movements (e.g., when infants switch from crawling to walking or when a woman becomes pregnant or wears a tight skirt or stiletto heels). New locomotor tasks require transfer from one situation to another (e.g., when infants face a flight of stairs for the first time or decide to climb out of their cribs). Even on a biomechanical level, muscle activation must be adapted continuously to the changing status of limbs and body (Bernstein, 1967; Lashley, 1960; MacKay, 1982). In each case, adaptive locomotion requires the continual monitoring of and flexible alignment between what we are doing now and the movements required for what to do next (e.g., Gibson, 1966, 1979; Lee, 1994).

Older children and adults are expert at navigating everyday situations. They judge correctly whether stairs are too high for walking upright (Mark, 1987; Mark & Vogele, 1987; Pufall & Dunbar, 1992; Warren, 1984), whether doorways are too narrow to pass through frontward (Warren & Whang, 1987), and whether upward slopes are too steep for maintaining balance (Fitzpatrick, Carello, Schmidt, & Corey, 1994; Kinsella-Shaw, Shaw, & Turvey, 1992).

6

For such well-practiced actions, experts can determine what actions are possible on the basis of brief exploratory glances involving subtle movements of eyes, head, and body.

Even adult experts, however, are challenged by changes in their body dimensions or changes in their ability to maintain balance (Lee & Lishman, 1975). For example, when adults' body dimensions were altered by wearing platform shoes, they needed to make more exploratory movements to judge adequate chair heights for sitting (Mark, Baillet, Craver, Douglas, & Fox, 1990). After taking a few steps in their platform shoes, swaying slightly back and forth and moving their eyes and heads, adults quickly recalibrated judgments of adequate chair heights to their newly elongated bodies. When information obtained from exploratory movements was reduced by standing very still or looking through a small peephole, judgments were poor. Likewise, when forced to stand in an unaccustomed pose (heels together, toes out), participants moved quite a lot to maintain balance, but judgments were poor. Results indicate that exploratory stepping and swaying movements yielded information about altered body dimensions and their relevance for sitting. Adults knew how to explore when they were allowed to stand in a customary position but not when forced to maintain an awkward pose.

Furthermore, recalibration to altered information may be task specific. A series of clever experiments manipulated the concordance of visual information and mechanical, muscle information relevant to locomotor movements (Rieser, Pick, Ashmead, & Garing, 1995). Adults walked on a motorized treadmill dragged on a rolling platform behind a small truck. The treadmill and the truck could move at different speeds. Sometimes participants walked faster than the truck, with the result that muscle movements specified more effort than visual information from optic flow, and sometimes they walked more slowly than the truck, with the result that muscle movements specified less work than visual information. Results showed that participants recalibrated to the new state of affairs by systematically overestimating distance traveled after moving faster than the truck and underestimating distance traveled after moving more slowly than the truck. Most striking, learning transferred to new locomotor tasks involving forward locomotion but not to locomotor tasks involving sideways rotations. The findings suggest that learning was not specific to the particular muscle movements involved but that it was specific to the sorts of information that the movements generated (i.e., translation vs. rotation).

Like the adults in Mark et al.'s (1990) study, infants' body dimensions change dramatically over the first two years of life (e.g., Palmer, 1944). Beginning crawlers and walkers often find themselves perched in unstable new positions with attention focused on the immediate problem of maintaining balance. Further, like the adults in Rieser et al.'s (1995) experiments, babies must transfer information obtained in one situation to new locomotor tasks.

A striking example is the transition from crawling to walking. Most infants have extended experience crawling around on four limbs, but we know little about how infants adjust to a higher vantage point and increased balance requirements when they switch from crawling to walking upright.

As described below, information for guiding adaptive locomotion is multimodal and available through various exploratory movements: looking by moving eyes, head, and body, swaying in place or while locomoting, touching with hands and feet, and testing various locomotor options to observe the consequences. Typically, information-gathering movements are quite subtle and may be executed without conscious awareness. This seems especially true for brief looking and swaying movements. On the other hand, some forms of exploration appear quite concerted and deliberate, such as probing the surface with a hand or foot or testing various locomotor options. The following sections review previous research on infants' ability to obtain relevant information from exploratory movements and to adapt locomotor responses on the basis of the information obtained.

INFORMATION FOR A CONTINUOUS PATH: DISRUPTIONS IN VISIBLE SURFACE TEXTURE

A critical requirement for human locomotion is a continuous ground surface to support the body. Locomotion is impossible without a path, and this is one of the first facts of locomotion to which infants respond adaptively.

Continuous visual texture gradients provide information about a continuous path. Abrupt discontinuity in visible texture specifies the end of a path terminating at the edge of a sheer drop-off. Visual texture gradients shift abruptly from the larger optic elements on the path to the smaller optic elements far below at the floor of the crevice. Motion parallax also specifies depth at an edge because head movements cause slower flow of the farther optic texture elements compared to the closer texture elements visible directly beneath infants' hands or feet.

Dozens of studies have shown that crawling infants balk at the edge of an apparent drop-off on a "visual cliff" (e.g., Gibson & Walk, 1960). The classic arrangement is a Plexiglas table divided by a low starting platform. A textured checkerboard pattern is stretched directly beneath the "shallow" side of the table and 4 feet below the "cliff" side of the table (e.g., Walk & Gibson, 1961). Parents stand on first one side of the table and then the other side and coax their infants to cross. Although locomotion is perfectly safe in either direction over the sturdy Plexiglas surface, visual information on the shallow side specifies a continuous path, while visual information on the cliff side specifies a sheer drop-off to the floor of the crevice.

The critical information triggering infants' avoidance responses appears to be the abrupt discontinuity of visible texture along the path. Haptic information, available by touching the glass, specifies a firm, continuous surface either way. Babies did explore the cliff side by touching, but the lack of confirming visual information specifying a continuous path typically outweighed the haptic evidence, and most infants refused to cross (Gibson & Walk, 1960). A fishnet stretched directly beneath the glass on the cliff side provides sparse, visible texture for a continuous path, like a city subway grating or metal-latticed bridge. When confronted with this modified visual cliff, crawlers hesitated but eventually crossed, despite a view of the floor between the strands of netting (Gibson & Schmuckler, 1989). Faced with a homogeneous gray surface placed at various distances beneath the Plexiglas (0, 10, 20, or 40 inches), infants were equally likely to cross to their mother or to avoid going regardless of the height of the drop-off (Walk, 1966). Likewise, when presented with a matte, black surface, both crawling and walking infants eventually crossed after long latencies, but infants preferred a patterned surface with visible texture over the textureless black one in forced-choice tasks (Gibson et al., 1987).

Some species avoid a sheer drop-off from birth, but others require a period of locomotor experience. For example, precocial (already locomotor) infant goats and chickens avoided the deep side of a visual cliff in their first day of life (Gibson & Walk, 1960). Likewise, dark-reared hooded and albino rats avoided the deep side on first emerging from the dark. In contrast, dark-reared kittens walked over the apparent drop-off at first but showed increasing avoidance with each day of locomotor experience in the light (Walk & Gibson, 1961). The kittens did not learn to avoid the drop-off from experience on the visual cliff (which is, in fact, perfectly safe for locomotion) or from experience falling from a steep place. Rather, avoidance of the precipice depended on experience observing the visual consequences of self-locomotion on a continuous path (Held & Hein, 1963).

Like experiments with kittens, studies controlling for duration of locomotor experience indicate that human infants may learn to relate discontinuity in visible texture to consequences for locomotion. A cross-sectional experiment with 6–9-month-olds showed that most babies with fewer than 2 weeks of crawling experience crossed the visual cliff but that most infants with more than 6 weeks of crawling experience steadfastly refused to go (Bertenthal & Campos, 1984; Bertenthal, Campos, & Barrett, 1984). Longitudinal observations also point to the important role of locomotor experience in avoidance behavior on the cliff (Campos, Hiatt, Ramsay, Henderson, & Svejda, 1978). In their first few weeks of crawling, infants engaged in long periods of visual exploration from the starting platform but crossed the deep side of the cliff nonetheless. The same infants avoided the deep side after 4–16 weeks of crawling experience.

Frequent testing on the visual cliff is problematic, however, because babies eventually learn that transparent surfaces do provide support for locomotion (Titzer, 1995). In Campos et al.'s (1978) longitudinal study, for example, avoidance became attenuated in some experienced crawlers, and others innovated a compromise strategy. After long latencies, infants crossed the visual cliff, but they detoured along the wooden supports at the side of the platform, where visible texture was available, rather than crawling over the glass in the middle of the platform.

Heart-rate measures provide additional evidence for the role of locomotor experience in detecting a ground to support the body (e.g., Bertenthal & Campos, 1987; Bertenthal et al., 1984; Campos et al., 1992). Before infants began crawling, their heart rates decreased as they were lowered toward the deep side of the cliff, suggesting that they noticed the disparity in depth. (In fact, infants show depth perception in reaching tasks months before they begin crawling.) After 5–7 days of home crawling experience, infants' heart rates—a measure associated with wariness or fear—increased. When precrawling babies were given 30–40 hours of locomotor experience wheeling around their homes in mechanical baby-walkers, their heart rates also increased as they were lowered toward the drop-off. Real crawlers with 5–7 days of crawling and 30–40 hours of baby-walker experience showed the most accelerations in heart rate, termed a *double-dose* of experience by the authors (Campos et al., 1992). Note, however, that fearful heart rates do not translate directly into avoidance responses. The finding that fearful heart rates precede adaptive avoidance responses by several weeks suggests a progression from depth sensitivity to understanding the relevance of a drop-off for locomotion.

Further, learning may be specific to infants' typical method of locomotion. Real crawlers with several weeks of home crawling experience avoided traversal when facing the drop-off in a crawling position, but the same babies crossed the cliff moments later when supported upright in mechanical baby-walkers (Rader, Bausano, & Richards, 1980). This within-subject manipulation suggests that infants' knowledge about a path to support the body did not transfer automatically from independent crawling on four limbs to a new upright posture in a baby-walker where the machine provided balance and support. Apparently, both precrawlers and bona fide crawlers perceive depth at the edge. However, only infants having experience with a particular method of locomotion relate the depth of the drop-off to consequences for that locomotor method.

Summary: Information for a Continuous Path

Results across studies indicate that prelocomotor infants show sensitivity to disparity in depth, relatively inexperienced crawlers show fearful heart rates, and relatively experienced crawlers eventually avoid a sheer drop-off.

Although studies controlling for locomotor experience indicate that adaptive responding is related to crawling experience, there are no data about the crucial components of infants' everyday experience that may lead to avoidance responses. Some investigators have suggested that experience peering over drop-offs may facilitate learning (Thelen & Smith, 1994) or that experience falling over a drop-off may spur learning (Walk, 1966). However, there is no research describing the content of home crawling experience and no empirical evidence linking avoidance responses on the visual cliff with falling over a precipice at home (Scarr & Salapatek, 1970). In fact, most parents are extremely vigilant and protect newly mobile infants from falling by gating household stairs and rescuing them before they crawl off the bed or changing table.

Although some studies found evidence that maturational factors may also play a role, age and experience were confounded. Walk (1966), for example, found that older crawlers (older than 9.5 months) avoided the visual cliff, but these infants had many weeks of crawling experience and/or older ages at crawling onset. Rader and her colleagues (Rader et al., 1980; Richards & Rader, 1981, 1983) found that infants who began crawling at very young ages (before 6.5 months) crossed the cliff more than babies who began crawling at older ages, but infants in both early and late onset groups were relatively old at testing (9–12 months), and all had at least 30 days of experience. Statistical comparisons of Rader's data may have shown the strongest effects for onset age because the percentage of infants avoiding the visual cliff asymptotes with test age and experience (Bertenthal & Campos, 1984). Moreover, these cross-sectional comparisons are difficult to interpret because test age, locomotor experience, and onset age are linearly related and at least two measures tended to be highly correlated.

INFORMATION FOR A PATH TO FIT THE BODY: OBSTACLES AND APERTURES

Locomotion requires a sufficiently open path to fit the body. Although crawling and walking are impossible through obstructions, smooth steering around obstacles and through apertures is surprisingly slow to develop.

Visual information specifies the difference between an opening and an obstacle (Gibson, 1979). Head-on approach toward an opening results in an expanding vista, progressively revealing more and more background texture through the aperture. Approach toward an obstacle results in optic expansion of the outer contours of the impasse, progressively occluding more and more background texture until the object fills the visual field. Rate of expansion in optic flow provides information specifying the speed of travel and the time to impending contact with the approaching surface (e.g., Lee, 1974, 1980). Likewise, the streaming pattern of optic texture elements provides information for steering a path through apertures and around obstacles (e.g., Lee & Thompson, 1982; Warren, Blackwell, Kurtz, Hatsopoulos, & Kalish, 1991; Warren, Mestre, Blackwell, & Morris, 1991; Warren, Morris, & Kalish, 1988). Steering along a straightaway results in a central locus of optic flow with symmetrical rate of expansion to all sides; steering a curved path results in a locus to one side with faster expansion of optic texture elements along the inner edge of the curve.

Many creatures exhibit sensitivity to visual information when searching for a clear path to fit the body (Schiff, 1965). Even frogs detect visual information that allows them to head for open ground as opposed to beating their heads on a solid wall (Ingle & Cooke, 1977). When lured through openings varying in width, frogs hopped through wide apertures large enough to fit their bodies but not through openings narrower than their largest body dimensions. Likewise, seabirds show sensitivity to visual information revealing time to collision (Lee & Reddish, 1981). Recordings on high-speed film showed that gannets soared downward with open wings for steering, then folded their wings prior to diving under the surface of the water. The timing of wing movements was closely calibrated with speed of travel and distance to the water.

Human infants show sensitivity to visual information specifying obstacles and apertures long before the onset of independent locomotion (Yonas, 1981). Three-month-olds pushed their heads backward when faced with impending collision with a solid, looming panel but leaned forward when faced with an approaching panel with a window cut out (Carrol & Gibson, 1981). The solid panel and the window were identical in size to equate visual expansion rate. Thus, differences in visual information were due only to the occlusion or disocclusion of background texture. Infants were more aroused by and oriented their bodies and arms toward the approaching obstacle, but they more passively watched the approaching opening.

Like the hopping of frogs and the diving of seabirds, human locomotion involves more complex responses than simple head movements for coping with obstructions in the path. Expert adult and child walkers turn sideways to fit through a narrow doorway, step over an obstacle near the ground, crawl under a barrier threatening overhead clearance, detour around an impassable obstacle, and so on. Experts' judgments were based on the geometric relation between aperture dimensions and the dimensions of their bodies. Adults executed subtle adjustments in walking as they approached doorways by rotating their shoulders as aperture width narrowed to shoulder width (Warren & Whang, 1987). Likewise, preschoolers negotiated obstacles by stepping over barriers lower than leg length, crawling under barriers lower than waist height, stooping under barriers lower than standing height, and walking normally under barriers with sufficient overhead clearance (Burton, Pick, Heinrichs, & Greer, 1989; Heinrichs, Bigbee, & Pick, 1991).

In contrast to the fluid and varied movements available to expert walkers, the repertoires of newly mobile infants are less flexible when coping with obstacles in the path. Adaptive locomotion may depend in part on learning that a variety of options can satisfy task demands and that each locomotor method is only a means for getting from here to there. When infants first begin crawling, they are stymied by an impassable barrier blocking the straightaway path. Newly mobile infants crawled up to a large barrier and persisted in futile attempts to go over it (Lockman, 1984). After several weeks of crawling experience, infants executed smooth detours around the barrier. In a forced-choice task, 10–13-month-old crawlers consistently chose a wide, 12-inch doorway over impassable 2- and 4-inch-wide apertures (Palmer, 1987). However, when dimensions were more similar (e.g., 8 inches vs. 12 inches), responses were indiscriminate, and infants crawled toward either opening.

Beginning walkers' gait is unstable and lurching, requiring a wider path of progression relative to body dimensions. Toddlers' balance is especially poor during periods of single-limb support (Bril & Breniere, 1992b), and options such as stepping over barriers or stooping to pass under them may therefore await improvements in postural control and leg strength. Inexperienced 13-month-old walkers adjusted their gait more often (decreased step length and velocity, increased body rotation) and took more detours approaching narrow doorways than they did approaching wide ones (Palmer, 1987). More experienced 13-month-olds made fewer adjustments in walking patterns, suggesting a more controlled, narrower path of progression. In addition, novice walkers were more likely to walk up to the impasse and touch the sides of the doorway with their hands, but experienced walkers adjusted their gait before arriving at the obstruction.

Likewise, infants' age and walking experience were related to their ability to negotiate low hurdles blocking the path or doorways threatening overhead clearance. Twenty-four-month-olds stepped successfully over higher hurdles than did less experienced 12- and 18-month-olds, and the older, more experienced children were less likely to misjudge possible hurdle heights and bump into the obstacle (Schmuckler, 1996). However, error rates, even in the most expert group, did not drop below 50% until hurdles were nearly twice as high as infants' highest successful hurdle. More experienced 16-month-olds coped with changes in overhead clearance by stooping and detouring (Palmer, 1989b). Less experienced 13-month-olds were more likely to revert to crawling through the lower doorways.

Summary: Obstacles and Apertures

Prelocomotor infants respond differentially to obstacles and apertures. However, moving the head forward or backward in response to a looming

13

panel does not approximate the complexity and effort of executing adaptive locomotor responses. Coping with obstacles and apertures is linked loosely with infants' age and locomotor experience. Infants appear to make finer distinctions between obstacle/aperture size and acquire skills for modifying gait patterns as they get older and make more independent trips through the environment.

Age-related changes toward the end of the first year may contribute to improved performance on tasks involving detours from the straightaway path (Rieser, Doxsey, McCarrell, & Brooks, 1982). Detours are associated with a decrease in perseverative errors in object search tasks (Lockman, 1984) and may rely on means-ends analyses, planning, or the ability to consider multiple options simultaneously (Willatts, 1989).

On the other hand, infants' poor performance on obstacle/aperture tasks may result from the minimal consequences of errors. In contrast to the practical constraints on locomotion found in birds and frogs, there are no dire consequences from infants' futile attempts to go through an impassable obstacle. Infants' crawling and walking steps are slow compared with the rapid flight of plummeting gannets, and infants can move forward and backward in contrast to the unidirectional locomotion of hopping frogs. Adaptive responding for infants involves minimizing path length or motor output rather than choosing between safe and dangerous routes. With no pressing urgency to optimize outcome and avoid errors, improvements may take many months to appear. In addition, age and experience are correlated with increased locomotor proficiency, and subtle modifications in gait may therefore require sufficient postural control for execution.

VISUAL INFORMATION FOR MAINTAINING BALANCE

Locomotion requires more than a continuous ground and sufficient space to fit the body. Infants must also maintain balance. Even standing quietly on flat ground requires compensatory sways to keep balance. To a casual observer, infants may appear motionless when balanced in a sitting, crawling, or standing position. However, the body continually rocks gently forward and backward as the center of mass shifts over the base of support. In general, balance control is more difficult for infants than for adults because, like balancing a short stick as opposed to a long one on the fingertips, infants' shorter bodies topple faster and require quicker corrections (Forssberg & Nashner, 1982; McCollum & Leen, 1989). Dynamic balance while moving forward poses additional problems. While moving, infants' bodies are upheld over a smaller base of support—one hand and one knee during crawling and one foot during walking. Moreover, infants must initiate disequilibrium and then recapture balance in rapid succession to keep moving forward (Breniere, Bril, & Fontaine, 1989; Bril & Breniere, 1992a).

Elegant experiments show that patterns of optic flow provide visual information important for maintaining balance—we literally see ourselves sway forward and backward (e.g., Gibson, 1979; Lee & Thompson, 1982; Lishman & Lee, 1973). The typical arrangement is a "moving room." The floor of the room is stationary, but the front and/or side walls glide forward or backward on bicycle wheels, simulating the patterns of optic flow generated by compensatory sways to keep balance. Amusement park rides and Omnimax cinemas use similar techniques to simulate the visual consequences of self-locomotion.

When the walls in a moving room roll forward, the forward stream of optic texture elements simulates the visual consequences of a backward sway of the body. When the walls roll backward, the backward stream of optic flow simulates the visual consequences of a forward sway of the body. Movement of the front wall creates a radial flow structure, and optic texture elements stream outward from a central point of expansion. Movement of the side walls creates a lamellar flow structure, and optic texture elements stream in parallel along the sides of the path.

Adults standing in a moving room shifted weight forward and backward like puppets in accordance with simulated visual flow (e.g., Lee, 1980; Lee & Lishman, 1975; Stoffregen, 1985). When the walls rolled forward, participants perceived themselves swaying backward, and they instigated forward steps or sways in response. When the flow streamed backward, participants perceived themselves rocking forward, and they instigated backward sways or staggers in response. Moreover, adults responded to the structure of visual information rather than its location on the retina (Stoffregen, 1985). With their eyes pointed frontward so that radial flow from the front wall falls in the center of the retina and lamellar flow from the side walls falls on the periphery, adults adjusted posture only for movement of the side walls. With heads turned sideways so that radial flow from the front wall now fell on the periphery of the retina and lamellar flow from the side wall fell on the center, adults still adjusted posture only for movement of the side walls.

Prelocomotor infants show early signs of sensitivity to visual flow information pertinent to balance control. Two-month-olds moved their heads backward in response to visual flow in a moving room (Butterworth & Pope, 1983, cited in Bertenthal & Clifton, in press), and 9-month-olds seated in a canvas sling exerted backward pressure with their whole bodies in response to backward movement of the front and side walls and forward pressure in response to forward movement of the walls (Bertenthal & Bai, 1989). Likewise, 7–12-month-olds seated on the floor of the moving room moved their torsos forward and backward in accordance with visual flow information from the front and side walls (Butterworth & Cicchetti, 1978; Butterworth & Hicks, 1977).

15

After infants can stand alone, they show improvements in responding to visual information for controlling balance. Younger, less experienced toddlers (10–24 months old) overcompensated for induced sway; they typically staggered or fell over in response to movement of either front or side walls (Bertenthal & Bai, 1989; Butterworth & Hicks, 1977; Lee & Aronson, 1974; Schmuckler & Gibson, 1989; Stoffregen et al., 1987). Older preschoolers (24–60 months old) maintained upright stance with small steps or compensatory swaying movements in the appropriate direction; they responded only to movements of the side walls. Likewise, walkers' (13–35 months old) posture was most perturbed in a moving hallway when they had the additional task of steering around obstacles instead of simply walking along a clear path; younger, less experienced children were more likely to stagger or topple over (Schmuckler & Gibson, 1989). Steering requires differentiation of radial from lamellar flow, and turning to avoid obstacles may challenge infants' already jeopardized balance.

Summary: Visual Information Pertinent to Balance

Sensitivity to visual information important for balance control precedes adaptive locomotor responses; after walking onset, improvements in compensatory responses to simulated sway are related to infants' age and locomotor experience. In this case, developmental factors may facilitate finer adjustments in standing posture and increased differentiation of one kind of optic flow from another (i.e., radial flow for steering from lamellar flow for controlling balance). Likely, with gains in muscle strength and increased coordination between body parts, infants' attention can shift from the immediate exigencies of maintaining balance to differences in the structure of optic flow for controlling actions a few steps ahead.

MECHANICAL INFORMATION FOR MAINTAINING BALANCE

Compensatory sway also generates mechanical information relevant to keeping balance by stimulating receptors in the soles of the feet, muscles, and joints and in the vestibular system. Infants can feel themselves as well as see themselves losing balance. In fact, beginning walkers (12–14 months old) initiate equal amounts of compensatory sway in the dark and in the light (Ashmead & McCarty, 1991; Woollacott, Debu, & Mowatt, 1987).

Typically, sensitivity to mechanical information for controlling balance is observed on a "moving floor" (e.g., Nashner & McCollum, 1985; Woollacott, Hofsten, & Rosblad, 1988). Participants sit, stand, or walk on an adjustable platform. The platform makes sudden discrete forward or backward translations or tilts, like tripping over a curb or standing on a subway car when it starts or stops. Compensatory muscle responses are recorded with surface EMG, and compensatory swaying movements may be measured with a force plate, an accelerometer, or high-speed motion analysis of anatomical landmarks.

Adults' muscle and sway responses to mechanical perturbations of posture are quick, fluid, and differentiated (e.g., Nashner, 1977; Nashner & McCollum, 1985; Woollacott & Jensen, 1992). Standing adults shifted weight forward or backward in accordance with the direction of floor movement by rotating around the hips or ankles. When the floor jerked their bodies forward, extensor muscles in the back of the legs and trunk activated, followed by flexor muscles on the front of the legs and trunk, to return their bodies to an upright position and minimize back and forth oscillations (Woollacott, 1986). When the floor jolted participants backward, muscles in the front of the legs and abdomen activated, followed by reciprocal enervation of extensor muscles on the back of legs and trunk. Even neck muscles participated in coping with moving floors by bringing the head back into upright position as the leg muscles did their work (Woollacott et al., 1988). Likewise, when adults sat on a stool, neck and trunk muscles worked in efficient synchrony to counteract sudden floor movements—extensor followed by flexor muscles to cope with a forward jerk and flexors followed by extensors to cope with a backward jerk (Woollacott, 1986).

Compared with adults, infants' muscle and sway responses to mechanical perturbations are slower, more variable, less smooth, and less differentiated. Research with very young, prelocomotor infants showed conflicting results for directionally appropriate muscle responses. Woollacott et al. (1987) found that the neck muscles of infants unable to sit alone fired indiscriminately in response to backward and forward perturbations and that the rest of their muscles lay inert or tensed simultaneously. Three- to 5-month-olds propped in an infant seat did not show directionally appropriate head and trunk compensations in response to sudden floor movements, although their neck muscles tensed after each jerk, but independent sitters (8–14 months) showed more adaptive, directionally appropriate neck and trunk muscle responses. In contrast, Hirschfeld and Forssberg (1994) found evidence of directionally appropriate muscle responses in infants unable to sit alone and independent sitters. Muscles on the front of infants' neck, trunk, and hips fired in response to backward perturbations in both groups, and muscles on the front also fired for forward perturbations in independent sitters.

Coping with a moving floor is most difficult when infants first begin standing, balancing, and taking steps. New walkers' (8–14 months) muscle and sway responses were indiscriminate and amorphous (Woollacott et al., 1987; Woollacott & Sveistrup, 1992). In contrast, older toddlers (15–24 months) and preschoolers (2–3 years) showed the same general pattern of lower to upper leg muscle responses as adults, and they initiated sways in the appropriate direction by rotating around their ankles (Forssberg & Nashner, 1982). However, young children's leg muscles responded sluggishly compared with those of adults, and trunk muscles lagged long behind leg muscles or did not fire at all (Shumway-Cook & Woollacott, 1985). In addition, preschoolers' flexors and extensors tended to co-contract, resulting in excessively large movements, stiff, undifferentiated, and long in duration. Finally, by the time children are 7–10 years old, their muscle reactions and motor output resemble the swift, efficient compensations of adults (Woollacott & Shumway-Cook, 1990).

Summary: Mechanical Perturbations of Balance

EMG recordings are difficult to collect and interpret in young children; existing research suffers from small samples and sparse data. However, three facts seem clear. First, infants are sensitive to mechanical information relevant to balance control prior to independent mobility; second, functionally adaptive sway responses precede adult-like muscle activation patterns; and, third, over the course of development, muscle response patterns become quicker and more differentiated, and sways become more directionally appropriate, quiet, and efficient.

INFORMATION OBTAINED FROM TOUCHING WITH HANDS AND FEET: SURFACE RIGIDITY AND FRICTION

An additional source of mechanical information for keeping balance comes from exploratory touching movements. However, unlike compensatory responses to sudden jerks or tilts of the supporting surface, exploratory touching functions like antennae, probing to obtain information about the ground ahead. Information obtained from touching is especially important for adapting locomotion to the rigidity and frictional properties of a ground surface. Differences in visible texture and luminance are not sure cues specifying whether a surface is substantial or slippery. Rather, these sorts of properties are best specified by observing the consequences of an event—observing the consequences from a distance, such as when a companion sinks to the waist in quicksand, or observing the consequences of a self-generated event, such as pressing one's own hands into the muck.

Touching a supporting surface with the hands or feet provides information by stretching and deforming the skin and by stimulating receptors in muscles and joints (e.g., Carello, Fitzpatrick, Domaniewicz, Chan, & Turvey, 1992; Gibson, 1962; Lederman & Klatzky, 1993). Pressure generated by a strong push or an aggressive rub can specify whether the surface will support infants' body weight and provide sufficient friction for forward locomotion. Rocking and stepping movements with the hands or feet may be especially relevant for balance control by generating torque at the wrists or ankles and shearing forces at the hands or feet. Typically, touching is accompanied by looking, and information relevant to balance control is therefore multimodal and redundant. For example, pressing the hands into a spongy ground surface generates both mechanical and visual flow information about surface resistance to shifts in infants' weight.

Adults' touches are remarkably efficient, and they become even more efficient with repeated experience over trials (Klatzky, Lederman, & Reed, 1989). Although adults show preferred ways of touching to obtain information about particular surface properties, most touching movements yield information about a variety of properties simultaneously (Lederman & Klatzky, 1987). For example, adults typically scrape an extended index finger along an object's surface to discriminate its texture but enclose an object in their hand to detect its shape and size. However, rubbing also yields sufficient information to detect rigidity and temperature, and enclosure also yields sufficient information to detect texture, rigidity, weight, and temperature. Given the option to explore by looking alone or by looking plus touching, adults used visual information to discriminate objects' size and shape but used looking plus touching to discriminate such material properties as texture, rigidity, temperature, and weight (Klatzky, Lederman, & Matula, 1993; Klatzky, Lederman, & Reed, 1987).

As with other sources of information, sensitivity to differences in rigidity and texture precedes the onset of mobility. For example, prelocomotor infants are sensitive to differences in rigidity specified visually and haptically by exploring with mouth and hands. One-month-olds looked longer at events involving pliant objects after sucking on a pliant pacifier, and they looked longer at events involving rigid objects after sucking on a hard, plastic pacifier (Gibson & Walker, 1984). Likewise, 1-month-olds showed differential looking at nubby and smooth objects after sucking on nubby or smooth pacifiers (Meltzoff & Borton, 1979). Once infants acquire skills for manipulating objects, they explore rigid and pliant ones, and nubby and smooth ones, differentially with their hands (Eppler, 1995; Palmer, 1989a; Rochat, 1987, 1989; Ruff, 1984).

Exploratory touching movements are available to both crawling and walking infants for obtaining information about a ground surface. However, crawlers' quadruped posture is remarkably stable over wide variations in surface rigidity and friction, and the consequences of coordinated looking and touching may therefore have little practical relevance before infants begin walking upright. Eight- to 15-month-old crawling infants, for example, differentiated between a pliant waterbed and a sturdy plywood surface by increased duration

19

of coordinated looking and touching (Gibson et al., 1987). Infants poked and pressed their hands into the waterbed and watched the consequent ripples. However, both surfaces were safe for quadruped locomotion, and crawlers crossed them both in equal numbers.

Upright posture is more easily disrupted by changes in surface rigidity and friction. Walking infants (10–21 months), too, differentiated between sturdy plywood and a pliant waterbed by increased touching and looking at the waterbed (Gibson et al., 1987). However, in contrast to crawlers, walkers preferred the rigid surface in forced-choice tasks, and they adapted locomotion by crawling rather than walking over the waterbed. Similarly, when presented with four differently textured 35° slopes, all descending from a central square platform, 11–19-month-old walkers explored surfaces by touching with hands and feet, and they selected the high-friction surfaces rather than the slippery ones for descent (Adolph et al., 1993b). Fourteen-month-old walking infants maintained an upright stance on high-friction rubber, greased plastic, and foam surfaces by using different manual control strategies (Stoffregen, Adolph, Thelen, Gorday, & Sheng, in press). On the high-friction surface, infants stood freely with their hands at their sides. On the slippery and foam surfaces, infants held onto supporting posts with one or both hands, especially while executing skating or bouncing movements with their legs. Some infants refused to stand on the challenging surfaces and sat down instead.

Summary: Information Obtained from Touching

Research on infant locomotion over surfaces varying in rigidity and friction points to three findings. First, sensitivity to rigidity and texture appears before the onset of independent locomotion, and both crawling and walking infants differentiate surface properties by exploratory touching movements. Typically, infants look while touching so that they can see as well as feel the consequences of exploratory probes.

Second, variations in rigidity and friction have very different practical consequences for crawling infants than they do for walking infants. Crawling is stable on pliant or slippery surfaces, but walking is not. Accordingly, there is no evidence that crawlers adapt locomotion for travel over such surfaces, but relatively old and experienced walkers prefer firm and high-friction surfaces to pliant or slippery ones, and they adapt locomotor methods to maintain balance. It is possible that adaptive responding awaits a point in development when locomotion is challenged by variations in rigidity and friction.

Third, walking infants are not limited to subtle hip or ankle rotations in order to maintain upright balance. Although such subtle movements may take many months to develop for coping with sudden movements in the floor, other quite practical responses are available in more everyday situations. If infants feel themselves losing balance, they can take compensatory steps forward or backward, grip a handrail for additional support, or simply refuse to cooperate by sitting down.

INFORMATION OBTAINED FROM TESTING LOCOMOTOR OPTIONS AND OBSERVING THE CONSEQUENCES

Exploration in the service of locomotion may take a more straightforward form: testing locomotor options and observing the consequences. The most direct route to knowledge is to plunge in—like diving into a pool to test the water. Learning by doing is the quickest, surest way to obtain information. Although the direct approach is not so smart when the penalties incurred for making errors are high, most young infants are monitored closely by caregivers. Baby-proofed homes and vigilant parents may result in a safe arena in which infants can explore new locomotor methods and test their limits and efficacy in handling various locomotor tasks.

More circumspect testing of locomotor options can take the form of playful exploration or concerted means-ends exploration. Caregivers commonly remark on children's spontaneous exploration of various locomotor movements—pulling to a stand, then sitting down, then pulling to a stand again, seemingly for the sheer joy of mastery and movement; rolling and crawling, with varying speed and patterns back and forth over the same patch of floor; trying the playground slide in various breathtaking positions; social games that consist of different sequences of locomotor movements (e.g., Red Light–Green Light, Simon Says, and Follow the Leader).

Harlow and Mears (1978) called this sort of whole body, self-motion play *peragration*. Frequency of peragration in infant rhesus monkeys was six times higher than ordinary locomotion or visuotactile exploration of objects, as the monkeys leaped, jumped, ran, somersaulted, and tumbled in rooms empty of all but their playmates. A striking example was the determined efforts of one infant monkey to reach a bar and rings far above the floor. The infant gazed at a tiny 2-centimeter knob projecting from the wall and day after day leaped at the wall, higher and higher, until he finally caught hold of the little knob. From there, he chimneyed around the corner until reaching the bar and rings. Then, with his back pressed against the ceiling, the monkey gazed and chattered at the room below. Common to all these examples is the treatment of locomotor methods as means, separate and potentially independent from an explicit problem or end state.

Many authors have described more sober means-ends exploration in tasks involving objects or surfaces as tools (e.g., Leeuwen, Smitsman, & Leeu-

21

wen, 1994; Willatts, 1989). Piaget's (1952) children, for example, explored various ways of dropping objects to obtain a satisfying noise and, through test and effort, discovered that a cloth or string could be used to drag another object into reach. Kohler's (1925) chimps devised various means of trans-forming sticks into rakes or vaulting poles to reach fruit lures outside their cage or hung from the ceiling. Similarly, McGraw (1935) provides wonderful descriptions of means-ends exploration in locomotor and object problem solving as one infant coped with stacking boxes, combining sticks, and so on to capture his prizes.

More recently, Ulrich, Thelen, and Niles (1990) tempted crawling and walking infants (8–25 months) with colorful toys placed at the top of three different staircases (3-inch, 6-inch, and 12-inch risers). Younger infants (younger than 18 months of age) tended to ignore the 12-inch stairs, but older infants (over 18 months) tried all three staircases equally often. In the under-18 group, babies with more walking experience and more exposure to stairs at home tried the 6-inch stairs more often than less experienced youngsters, but, in the older group, walking and stair-climbing experience did not predict babies' responses. Most illuminating, however, was infants' spontaneous exploration of various means of utilizing the stairs. Infants some-times headed straight for the toys, but most babies also crossed from one staircase to another, climbed repeatedly up and down, or turned in full circles on the steps. Playful peragration was especially evident in the older (over 18 months) group.

Summary: Testing Locomotor Strategies and Positions

Infancy is rife with examples of playful and concerted exploration of vari-ous locomotor movements and postures. In the context of explicit problem solving, this sort of peragration may take on the character of means-ends exploration, where infants test various locomotor methods by shifting posi-tions, similar to the construct described by Piaget (1952). However, despite experimenters' best-laid plans, infants' motivation for performing means-ends exploration in locomotor tasks may be mastery or sheer joy of moving. Infants' criteria for judging the riskiness or immediacy of a situation may be different from those of adults. Babies may sometimes plunge in when more wary adults would pursue more cautious options. And infants sometimes make tasks more energy consuming than need be, especially when the practi-cal consequences are not pressing. In tasks such as going up stairs, steering through apertures, and detouring around obstacles, infants are apparently unconcerned with optimizing outcomes. The goal may be more playful or information gathering. This point is more striking in research comparing in-fants' ascent and descent of slopes.

LOCOMOTION OVER SLOPES

Slopes are an ideal venue for studying adaptive locomotion in infants for several reasons. First, slopes are novel, allowing firsthand observation of how infants learn to cope with an unfamiliar ground surface. Newborns are sensitive to differences in the slant of visible objects (Atkinson, Hood, Wattam-Bell, Anker, & Tricklebank, 1988; Slater & Morison, 1985; Slater, Morison, & Somers, 1988), and older, prelocomotor babies adjust their hand position to grasp objects slanting in different orientations (Hofsten & Fazel-Zandy, 1984; Lockman, Ashmead, & Bushnell, 1984). However, most babies have few opportunities to learn about slanted *ground* surfaces in everyday situations. In addition, parents typically limit exposure to other ascent and descent tasks throughout their infants' first year of life by gating household stairs and closely monitoring babies after they discover how to clamber on and off furniture.

Second, the task is ripe for examining the informational basis of adaptive responses. Slopes share many of the virtues but few of the problems of other locomotor tasks in the literature. Similar to a visual cliff, slopes involve a disparity in depth between the summit and the floor. As infants peer over the edge, their movements generate motion parallax and yield visual information about postural stability, surface slant, frictional properties, and the dimensions of the hill. However, in contrast to the situation with the visual cliff, on slopes, visual information and haptic information are in accord rather than in conflict, and the ground surface has a continuous visible texture rather than a discrete break in the path. As in the moving room, infants can obtain visual information about their own postural stability from swaying movements on the starting platform prior to crossing the brink. However, in contrast to the moving room, the effects of optic flow are harder to infer.

Similar to deciding between locomotion over compliant waterbeds and rigid plywood, coordinated looking and touching are excellent sources of information for controlling balance on slopes. In fact, adults can detect subtle differences in possibilities for walking up hills from visual information and exploratory probes with their feet, hands, or handheld canes. Adults judged correctly when a large visible ramp was the same slant as a small hidden ramp they felt with a foot, and participants' judgments of whether they could walk up hills closely matched their actual abilities (Kinsella-Shaw et al., 1992). Likewise, adults matched a hidden palm board to the slant of a real, outdoor hill (Proffitt, Bhalla, Gossweiler, & Midgett, 1995). Blindfolded adults even judged correctly whether they could balance on uphill slopes by poking the surface with a handheld cane (Fitzpatrick et al., 1994). However, unlike waterbeds, slopes challenge balance control in both quadruped and upright postures, providing a more stringent test of adaptive responses in crawlers and walkers.

As with detour, aperture, and stair-climbing tasks, there are multiple, viable options for coping with slopes. Means-ends exploration can yield information useful in selecting an appropriate climbing or sliding position. In addition, slopes may provide a better test case for assessing adaptive responding. The apparent consequences of falling on downhill slopes are aversive compared with detour, aperture, or stair-climbing tasks, with the result that infants are more likely to demonstrate their most accurate judgments when faced with that particular challenge.

Finally, slant can vary continuously in an experimental arrangement, allowing precise measurement of infants' physical abilities and judgments. Ability to locomote successfully on slopes depends on their steepness and on whether the goal is to go up or down. The role of steepness is straightforward—steeper hills are more challenging because balance control is more difficult—but the effects of direction of movement may require some explanation.

Biomechanical and Practical Constraints on Going Up as Opposed to Going Down

Because of the configuration of the human body relative to the configuration of upward and downward hills, ascent and descent are very different sorts of tasks. Going uphill is easier than going down.

Biomechanically, going uphill is tiring but relatively easy to control. It takes more energy to hoist limbs upward (Dean, 1965) because gravity constrains forward momentum from step to step. However, slower movements allow more time to maneuver limbs into the appropriate position. As shown in Figure 1, infants support their weight on a fully extended leg or arm so that muscles contract to exert force. Walkers' moving leg, and crawlers' moving arm, contacts the hill in a flexed position partway through the swing cycle, and placement is not critical for keeping balance. The consequences of mishaps are minimal because infants' hands are in a good position to stop a fall. Moreover, there are sound biomechanical reasons for walkers to attempt a running start on steep hills. On two feet, there is more vertical force to counteract slippage than when body weight is spread over hands and feet (Hudson & Johnson, 1976; Walker, 1989).

In contrast, going downhill is less tiring (Dean, 1965) but more difficult to control (Nelson & Osterhoudt, 1971). Infants must curb forward momentum either by taking small, slow steps and bracing between them or by racing down the hill and braking on flat ground at the bottom (Adolph, Gill, Lucero, & Fadl, 1996; McGraw, 1935). Babies must support body weight and maintain balance on a bent arm or leg so that muscles must lengthen (requiring more strength) to exert force (Figure 1). The leading limb straightens

FIGURE 1.—*a*, Crawling and walking uphill. The supporting limb is fully extended, and the moving limb contacts the hill in a flexed position early in the swing cycle. The hands are in a good position to break a fall. *b*, Crawling and walking downhill. The supporting limb is flexed, and the moving limb contacts the hill fully extended and late in the swing cycle. The hands are in an awkward position to break a fall.

at the end of its swing cycle before contacting the slope, and its placement is critical for keeping balance. Both crawling and walking downhill leave infants' hands awkwardly positioned to break a fall, and the consequences of error can be quite serious (Adolph, 1995; Adolph, Eppler, & Gibson, 1993a).

Performance differences between ascent and descent begin early in life and continue throughout childhood (e.g., McCaskill & Wellman, 1938). For example, with a rigorous, daily training regime, one child crawled and walked up hills several weeks earlier than he mastered descending the same slopes (McGraw, 1935). At 9.5 months, he managed to crawl up 40° using his feet as propellers, and, at 20.8 months, he crawled up an incredible 70° on four limbs. Despite this daily training regime, the steepest hill he managed to crawl

25

down was 40° at 10.1 months. He walked up 32° at 13 months but did not walk down the same hill until 2 months later.

Without daily training, infants' achievements are more modest. When encountering slopes for the first time, crawling infants (8.5 months) and walking infants (14 months) managed hills in the 2°–30° range, and babies were more successful crawling and walking up hills than they were going down (Adolph, 1995; Adolph et al., 1993a). Preschool children showed the same pattern of results in more demanding beam-walking tasks (Adolph, Ruff, Cappozoli, & Kim, 1994; Giacalone & Rarick, 1985). Children walked faster and farther along upwardly slanting beams than along level or downwardly slanting beams. Variations in height and width of beams most disrupted performance during descent.

Adaptive Locomotion in Crawling and Walking Infants

Differential effects of task constraints on infants' physical ability represent only part of the story about slopes. Adaptive locomotion requires infants to match their method of travel to their own physical abilities relative to the degree of slant and the direction of traversal. In a series of experiments, my colleagues and I (Adolph, 1995; Adolph et al., 1993a; Eppler, Adolph, & Weiner, 1996) observed 8.5-month-old crawling infants and 14-month-old walking infants on a walkway with adjustable slope (0°–40°). Parents at the far end of the walkway encouraged their infants to come up or down, while an experimenter followed alongside infants to ensure their safety. The shallowest slopes were safe for crawling and walking, but the steepest hills required alternative methods of locomotion, such as clambering up on hands and knees, going down in various sliding positions, or avoiding traversal. Infants' actual, physical abilities on slopes were compared with the accuracy of their judgments and the duration of their exploratory activity on the starting platform.

On uphill trials, both crawlers and walkers charged up steep and shallow hills trial after trial, without hesitating or touching slopes from the starting platform. Many infants fell partway up steeper hills, but all safely caught themselves. Such learning by doing is actually a sensible solution for going uphill because there is little danger from falling. In fact, after falling on repeated attempts in the same trial, many infants eventually reached the summit.

On downhill trials, where consequences of falling are more serious, young crawlers' responses were clearly less discriminating than those of older walking infants. As in other locomotor tasks, differential exploration preceded adaptive responding. Tested on full-size slopes in the locomotor task, or seated in front of a large rotating palm board, 8–9-month-old crawlers explored steep hills more than shallow ones by increased looking and touching (Adolph et al., 1993a; Eppler et al., 1996). In both locomotor and nonlocomotor tasks, crawlers pressed their hands on and rocked at the top of steep slopes while looking at the surface and their hands. However, after prolonged exploration on impossibly steep full-size slopes, young crawlers went down headfirst nonetheless, requiring rescue by an experimenter. Crawlers never tested alternative means for descent, although every infant demonstrated the component movements for sliding down in prone, sitting, and backing positions prior to testing on slopes.

In contrast, older, 14-month-old walkers are expert at coping with descent. Toddlers select appropriate methods of locomotion according to the degree of slant. When tested on two slopes—a safe 10° hill and a risky 36° hill—with the height of the hills held constant, 14-month-old toddlers walked down the shallow hill and slid down or avoided the steep one (Eppler et al., 1996). Results indicate that toddlers responded to differences in slant per se because the height of the drop-off was constant. In fact, a few toddlers' subversive attempts to back off the rear of the starting platforms provided compelling evidence that responses were based on slant rather than vertical distance to the floor.

More impressive, 14-month-old walkers' exploration and locomotor responses are scaled closely to their physical ability to walk down slopes. In a recent experiment, Adolph (1995) used a psychophysical staircase procedure to estimate each child's walking ability on slopes (0°–36°). The staircase procedure determined the steepest hills infants could walk up and the steepest hills infants could walk down—their uphill and downhill *slope boundaries*. Trials were coded on-line as either success (walked safely), failure (tried to walk but fell), or refusal to walk (slid down, clambered up, or avoided going). Steeper hills were presented after successful trials and shallower hills after failures or refusals. The process continued until the experimenter identified a slope boundary to a 67% criterion. The slope boundary was the steepest hill the infant walked on two-thirds of trials and failed or refused on two-thirds of trials at the next 2° increment. Infants showed a wide range in their walking ability on slopes; boundaries ranged from 6° to 28°. Uphill and downhill slope boundaries were positively correlated, and measures of infants' walking proficiency on flat ground (e.g., step length, step width) were highly correlated with slope boundaries, indicating that estimates from the staircase procedure were reliable.

A *go ratio* ([successes + failures] / [successes + failures + refusals]) indexed adaptive responding on hills shallower and steeper than boundary. Perfect judgments would be indicated by a high ratio on hills shallower than boundary, where the probability of success was high, and a low ratio on slopes steeper than boundary, where alternative strategies were required. The informational basis of children's judgments was inferred from their exploratory activity on the starting platform: hesitating, touching, and testing different positions.

27

Results showed a close correspondence between infants' judgments and their walking boundaries on downhill slopes. Average go ratios were high, near 1.0, on hills shallower than infants' boundaries and decreased from 0.94 at slope boundary to 0.49 on slightly steeper slopes, to 0.23 on moderately steep slopes, and, finally, to 0.11 on impossibly steep slopes. Walkers' exploratory activity neatly mirrored their go ratios. Infants' latency and duration of touching increased with steeper, riskier hills. Walkers explored alternative means for descent by shifting positions on the starting platform, a response similar to means-ends exploration observed in object tasks (e.g., Piaget, 1952; Willatts, 1989). Shifts increased sharply on risky hills, and nearly all toddlers used a variety of sliding positions to go down.

In addition to measures of on-line exploratory activity, ongoing changes in duration of locomotor experience and locomotor proficiency also played a role in walkers' ability to cope with slopes. Duration of toddlers' everyday walking experience and measures of their walking proficiency on flat ground predicted adaptive responses on slopes (Adolph, 1995; Adolph et al., 1993a).

Summary: Slopes

Newborns are sensitive to differences in surface slant, and young, 8–9-month-old crawling infants differentiate downward hills by their spontaneous exploratory activity. However, cross-sectional comparisons between 8.5-month-old crawling infants and 14-month-old walking infants showed adaptive responding only in the older groups of walkers. Three separate experiments showed that walking infants tailored exploratory activity and method of locomotion to their level of walking proficiency on downward hills. Toddlers hesitated and touched hills at the limits of their walking abilities, and they slid down or avoided hills where probability of success was low. In addition, only the older walking infants displayed means-ends exploration by testing various options on the starting platform before going over the edge. Apparently, exploratory looking and touching movements appear prior to means-ends exploration of various locomotor methods and before infants relate information about downward slant to consequences for locomotion.

In contrast, infants in both groups were more reckless on uphill slopes. They attempted to crawl or walk up impossibly steep hills without prolonged exploration on the starting platform. The difference between uphill and downhill slopes in the older group of walkers indicates that infants treat ascent and descent as very different tasks, with very different practical consequences for locomotion.

III. IMPLICATIONS OF PREVIOUS RESEARCH AND THE PURPOSE OF THE CURRENT STUDY

AGE AND EXPERIENCE

Previous research showed developmental change in infants' ability to adapt locomotion to task constraints. In every task—visual cliffs, obstacles/apertures, moving rooms/floors, waterbed/plywood, stairs, and slopes—improvements were related to infants' age and/or duration of locomotor experience. Older, more experienced infants showed more appropriate, discriminating exploratory activity and more adaptive locomotor responses than younger, less experienced infants.

However, research on the development of adaptive locomotion is just beginning, and few investigators have tried to understand the separate effects of age-related and experience-related changes. The notable exception is research with infants on a visual cliff. The preponderance of data suggests that duration of crawling experience is the strongest predictor of adaptive responding. Studies that tested infants in their first few weeks of crawling showed that crawling experience predicted adaptive avoidance responses (Bertenthal et al., 1984; Campos et al., 1978). Likewise, studies that compared prelocomotor and locomotor infants' heart rates as they were lowered toward the drop-off found accelerated heart rates only in the experienced group. In contrast, studies showing a stronger statistical relation for crawling onset age or test age than for experience included only relatively experienced children in the sample (Richards & Rader, 1981, 1983; Walk, 1966). Bertenthal and Campos (1984) argued that these statistical analyses may be biased against experience if the relation between avoidance and experience is asymptotic rather than linear.

In either case, age and experience are not themselves explanatory factors. Age is only a crude substitute for other changes that drive improvements in locomotor tasks. For example, cognitive changes that accompany getting older may affect attention, information processing, or problem-solving abilities in locomotor situations. Likewise, duration of locomotor experience does

29

not explain adaptive responding without a theory of what infants learn from everyday crawling and walking experience and how they go about learning it.

BODIES, SKILLS, AND LOCOMOTOR STATUS

Age and experience are intercorrelated with changes in infants' body size, locomotor proficiency (crawling or walking skill), and locomotor status (whether infants are crawlers or walkers). Each of these factors may help mediate adaptive responding. Body dimensions, for example, affect the biomechanics of moving (Thelen, 1984). In particular, infants' overall body proportions and muscle-to-fat ratios are likely to affect their ability to obtain requisite information about the surface of support. Slimmer, more cylindrically shaped infants may have an easier time keeping their balance and executing exploratory movements than fatter, more top-heavy infants.

Locomotor proficiency refers to infants' current level of crawling or walking skill. Various gait measures, such as the size and speed of infants' crawling or walking steps, reflect infants' underlying balance control, interlimb coordination, and muscle strength (e.g., Bril & Breniere, 1992b). Improved levels of locomotor proficiency may affect the adaptiveness of infants' judgments by freeing up attentional resources or directing infants' attention to the relevant properties of the ground surface, just as an expert rock climber may notice handholds or footholds that a novice would not (e.g., Gibson, 1969).

Change in infants' locomotor status (whether infants are crawlers or walkers) may be important for adaptive responding because crawling and walking have different balance constraints and each posture affords different views of the ground ahead. Crawlers' posture is stable over many variations in terrain, and crawling infants have no practical urgency to switch from crawling to an alternative method of locomotion on a spongy or slippery ground surface (Gibson et al., 1987). In contrast, walkers' posture is challenged by pliant or slippery ground, and walking infants must choose alternative methods of locomotion to keep themselves from falling. The developmental transition in locomotor status from a more stable posture on four limbs to a less stable posture on two feet might trigger infants' attention to previously disregarded surface properties.

The literature provides scant data about effects of infants' bodies, skills, or locomotor status. However, my colleagues and I (Adolph, 1995; Adolph et al., 1993a) found that measures of infants' walking proficiency on flat ground predicted slope boundaries and judgments about risky slopes and that proficiency was a better predictor than walking experience. Although Adolph (1995) found no relation between body dimensions and infants' judgments about slopes, the range in infants' body size was quite small compared with the range in locomotor experience and proficiency. More intriguing, waterbed/plywood and slopes studies found differences according to infants' locomotor status. Crawlers attempted to crawl over waterbeds and risky slopes, but walkers adapted their method of locomotion. These results may be task specific because crawlers do behave adaptively on a visual cliff. Alternatively, the crawler/walker difference might result from an age or experience effect. In both waterbed and slopes tasks, crawlers were younger and less experienced than walkers.

HOW INFANTS ACQUIRE ADAPTIVE MOBILITY

In sum, previous research leaves central questions unanswered. Most important, what drives change in adaptive locomotion in infancy—infants' age, locomotor experience, body growth, locomotor proficiency, or locomotor status? Previous slopes research provides two clear end points for the developmental progression in adaptive responding: young, inexperienced crawlers behave indiscriminately on risky downhill slopes, but older, more experienced walkers respond adaptively. This *Monograph* seeks to understand the contribution of various developmental factors by observing the entire path of change between the end points identified in earlier studies. The current experiment employed a microgenetic method, tracking infants' performance on slopes on a trial-by-trial basis from their first crawling steps, over the transition from crawling to walking, to proficient walking several weeks later. This study is the first to examine transfer over the important transition from crawling to walking. In addition, the study used a complementary, developmental method to compare changing responses in the slopes task to ongoing changes in infants' age, experience, bodies, and skills.

The experimental design controlled for duration of locomotor experience, with the result that infants' ages varied within test sessions but all babies got older across sessions. If age were the primary predictor of change, then we would expect one smooth curve, from high error rates in early test sessions when infants were younger to low error rates in late test sessions when they were older. If locomotor status is the key to change, then we would expect two curves: a high, flat rate of errors across weeks of crawling and a lower error rate after the transition to walking. If locomotor experience were central for change, then we would expect two learning curves, from high to low errors over weeks of crawling and from high to low errors over weeks of walking. To assess the effects of general, everyday experience and those of specific experience on slopes, a control group, matched for general locomotor experience, was tested at key sessions (infants' first and tenth weeks of crawling and their first week of walking). Previous cross-sectional studies provided age-matched comparisons.

Adaptive locomotion requires on-line decision making, meaning that infants must use information obtained from exploratory movements to control locomotor responses. What is the developmental relation between exploratory movements and performance? Previous research indicates that prelocomotor infants are sensitive to information about surface properties that is relevant to balance control. At the earliest points in testing, crawling and walking infants showed the physical ability to execute exploratory looking, touching, and swaying movements. However, adaptive locomotor responses lagged behind differential exploration. Young crawlers, for example, showed high levels of visual and haptic exploration on risky slopes but attempted them nonetheless. The current study examined infants' looking and touching behavior on the starting platform in order to assess developmental changes in the amount of exploration and its functional outcome.

Adaptive locomotion also requires flexible means to achieve functional outcome. Where do new movements come from, and how do infants select among alternative options? In previous research, means-ends and detour behaviors appeared later developmentally than exploratory looking, touching, and swaying movements. Although these behaviors were not required for adaptive responding (infants could have simply avoided going), means-ends exploration and adaptive responses did appear at approximately the same time.

Possibly, means-ends testing may facilitate improvements in infants' judgments by helping babies discover and/or select new ways of coping. On slopes, for example, toddlers' means-ends shifts typically resulted in the selection of an alternative sliding position. On the other hand, means-ends behavior and variety in locomotor methods may be symptomatic of more general cognitive changes. Young crawlers, for example, may adhere more rigidly to a single course of locomotion because they are unable to inhibit rash responding (Diamond, 1990a, 1990b). Older infants may be better able to construct flexible, new methods to fit the task because of increased processing capabilities toward the end of the first year (e.g., Zelazo, 1982). The current study analyzed infants' movements on a trial-by-trial basis. In conjunction with parents' home diaries, it was possible to identify infants' first use of new locomotor methods and to chart their course after emergence in children's repertoires. Means-ends exploration was indexed by the number of shifts in position that infants made before starting onto slopes.

Finally, what are the effects of task constraints over development? Previous research suggests that infants may exhibit more errors in tasks where the practical consequences of errors are minimal. In particular, walking infants were more reckless on uphill than downhill slopes. The data suggest that infants may have little motivation to optimize energy expenditure, especially in arenas where there is little penalty for errors (e.g., aperture/obstacle tasks, climbing up stairs and uphill slopes). The design of the current study compared uphill and downhill slopes at each test session to assess developmental changes in infants' responses to different task constraints.

Chapters IV and V describe the logic of and the methods for assessing infants' performance in the slope task. Most important, the testing procedure allowed comparisons between changes in infants' physical ability to go up and down slopes and changes in the adaptiveness of infants' responses on safe and risky hills. Unlike traditional cognitive tasks where correct solutions are fixed (e.g., learning the rules of addition, learning about the conservation of quantities), adaptive responding in the slope task depended on infants' current level of locomotor proficiency. A risky hill one week was safe the next when crawling skill improved, and a slope that is safe for crawling might be risky for walking. Chapter VI charts the overall path of change over weeks of crawling and walking by describing group averages on safe and risky hills across test sessions. Chapter VII compares the relative contributions of experience, age, growth, and skill factors. Chapter VIII, the final empirical chapter, describes individual differences in infants' response patterns, providing an illustration of the range in normal development and additional information about the roles of developmental factors. The concluding chapter, Chapter IX, integrates current findings with results of previous research and presents a model for understanding the role of learning in infants' changing ability to navigate the everyday environment.

IV. METHOD

OVERVIEW

The overall plan of study was to fill in the gaps left by previous cross-sectional experiments (Adolph, 1995; Adolph et al., 1993a), particularly the important transition from crawling to walking. To observe the entire path of change, infants were tested longitudinally, from their first week of crawling until several weeks after they began walking. Primary outcome measures concerned the adaptiveness of infants' locomotor responses and the informational basis of infants' decisions. In addition, measures of ongoing developmental factors were compared with infants' behavior in the slopes task.

PARTICIPANTS

Twenty-nine healthy, full-term infants completed the study. Fourteen infants were firstborn, and the others had one or two older siblings. Most families were Caucasian and of middle-class socioeconomic status, and most parents were associated with Indiana University (eight were faculty, five staff, and seven students). All infants were raised by two parents. In two families, fathers were the primary caregivers, two infants stayed with their grandmothers during the day, and seven children went to group day care several days a week. One additional Korean family withdrew from the study because the parents spoke little English and had difficulty understanding procedures and scheduling sessions.

Families were recruited from published birth announcements, mother/baby classes, and referrals. Parents visited the laboratory with their infants before consenting to participate, and an experimenter verified infants' locomotor status. Two infants began crawling before they were recruited but were included in the sample because their first day of crawling was dated accurately from their mothers' calendars and home videotapes. Parents agreed to limit the babies' exposure to playground slides and to refrain from teaching infants

34

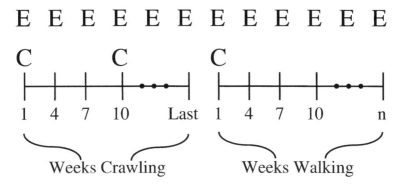

FIGURE 2.—Longitudinal design. Experimental-group infants (Es) were tested every 3 weeks; control-group infants (Cs) were tested only three times at matched sessions to control for experience with slopes in the laboratory. Ellipses represent a variable number of weeks.

how to go down household stairs for the duration of the study. However, most parents did coach their children in how to get down off furniture, turning infants' bodies into a backing position so that the infants could then scoot down feet first. Parents kept daily checklist diaries noting changes in infants' gross motor skills (sitting, standing, crawling, walking, and transitions between postures), serious falls, and experience going up and down home furniture and stairs. Families received T-shirts, diplomas, photograph albums, and videotapes as souvenirs of their participation.

Longitudinal Design

The study used a longitudinal design to control for duration of infants' crawling and walking experience. All infants were tested repeatedly, beginning when they first started to crawl and ending several weeks after they started to walk. As shown in Figure 2, 15 infants in an *experimental* group (seven girls, eight boys) were tested every 3 weeks to provide a continuous record of their ability to cope with slopes (this group is denoted by Es in the figure). Fourteen infants in a *control* group (seven girls, seven boys) were tested at three matched sessions (the first and tenth weeks of crawling and the first week of walking) to control for experience on slopes in the laboratory (this group is denoted by Cs in the figure). Dating from infants' first day of crawling and walking, test sessions were scheduled within 7 days before or after each target test day.

As shown in Figure 3, most experimental-group infants participated in the study for more than 10 months, and most control-group infants participated for more than 6 months (the total length of each bar represents duration of participation in the study). Experimental-group infants were between

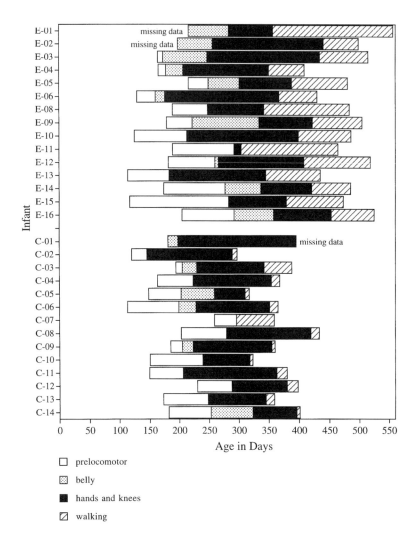

FIGURE 3.—Duration of participation in the study. The total length of bars represents the time that infants participated in the study. The length of each stacked bar represents duration of locomotor experience. Open bar = prelocomotor period; dotted bar = belly crawling; solid bar = crawling on hands and knees; striped bar = walking. Cases in which infants began crawling before they entered the study or in which they left the study before the onset of walking are denoted as *missing data*.

3.71 and 7.10 months old when they were recruited ($M = 5.6$ months) and between 13.5 and 17.2 months old ($M = 15.8$ months) at their last session. Controls were recruited when they were between 3.7 and 8.5 months old ($M = 5.7$) and were between 9.8 and 14.2 months old at their last session ($M = 11.8$). Fourteen experimental-group infants came for at least 10 weeks of walking, and seven of these babies participated for 13 or more weeks of walking. Most families' participation in the study ended in the same 2-month period, with the result that infants who began walking earlier tended to have more walking test sessions.

Overall, there were 215 uphill and 219 downhill complete protocols on slopes. Tables 1 and 2 show available slope data for each week of crawling and walking, respectively. Children missed few scheduled sessions, but the number of children contributing data to each session varied because some babies crawled longer than others or participated in the study for more weeks of walking. Most notably, seven experimental-group infants and four control-group infants missed part or all of their first crawling session. Two experimental-group infants had not yet been recruited (noted by "missing data" for E-01 and E-02 in Figure 3), one had a death in the family, one was sick, and three fussed partway through slope protocols. One control-group infant missed his first crawling session because he was sick, one fussed, and one fell asleep partway through slope protocols. Control-group infant C-07 never crawled and came at weeks 1 and 10 of walking instead. In addition, experimental-group infant E-11 was out of town from her thirteenth to her nineteenth weeks of walking. One control-group baby missed her scheduled walk session because her family moved away (noted by "missing data" for C-01 in Figure 3), and one control-group child missed his first walking session because he was sick but came at the next possible session time.

To include as much data as possible while maintaining the sample size above seven infants for presentation of group averages, infants' twenty-second or final week of crawling (if infants crawled longer than 22 weeks) was denoted as infants' "≥22d" crawling session (indicated by the final column in Table 1), and group averages are reported only up to the thirteenth week of walking.

Crawling and Walking Onset

The criteria for crawling and walking onset were quite strict in order to maximize the likelihood that infants would have the stamina to complete testing protocols on slopes from their first official onset day. *Crawling onset* was defined as the first day infants could travel 91 centimeters along a flat path (the horizontal length of the laboratory walkway) on three of four consecutive trials without falling or pausing for longer than 3 seconds between steps. Ses-

TABLE 1

CHILDREN CONTRIBUTING DATA TO UPHILL AND DOWNHILL TRIALS OVER WEEKS OF CRAWLING

WEEKS OF CRAWLING

Child's Number	1st U	1st D	4th U	4th D	7th U	7th D	10th U	10th D	13th U	13th D	16th U	16th D	19th U	19th D	22d U	22d D	25th U	25th D	28th U	28th D	31st U	31st D	34th U	34th D	37th U	37th D	≥22d U	≥22d D
Experimental group:																												
E-01	✓	✓	✓	✓	✓	✓	✓	✓	✓	✓	✓	✓	✓	✓	✓	✓											✓	✓
E-02	✓	✓	✓	✓	✓	✓	✓	✓	✓	✓	✓	✓	✓	✓	✓	✓	✓	✓	✓	✓	✓	✓	✓	✓	✓	✓	✓	✓
E-03	✓	✓	✓	✓	✓	✓	✓	✓	✓	✓	✓	✓	✓	✓	✓	✓	✓	✓	✓	✓	✓	✓	✓	✓			✓	✓
E-04	✓	✓	✓	✓	✓	✓	✓	✓	✓	✓	✓	✓	✓	✓	✓	✓	✓	✓	✓	✓							✓	✓
E-05	✓	✓	✓	✓	✓	✓	✓	✓	✓	✓	✓	✓	✓	✓	✓	✓	✓	✓	✓	✓							✓	✓
E-06		✓	✓	✓	✓	✓	✓	✓	✓	✓	✓	✓	✓	✓	✓	✓	✓	✓									✓	✓
E-08	✓	✓	✓	✓	✓	✓	✓	✓	✓	✓	✓	✓	✓	✓	✓	✓											✓	✓
E-09		✓	✓	✓	✓	✓	✓	✓	✓	✓	✓	✓	✓	✓	✓	✓											✓	✓
E-10	✓	✓	✓	✓	✓	✓	✓	✓	✓	✓	✓	✓	✓	✓														
E-11			✓	✓	✓	✓	✓	✓	✓	✓	✓	✓	✓	✓														
E-12			✓	✓	✓	✓	✓	✓	✓	✓	✓	✓	✓	✓														
E-13					✓	✓	✓	✓	✓	✓	✓	✓																
E-14					✓	✓	✓	✓																				
E-15	✓	✓	✓		✓	✓	✓	✓																				
E-16									✓	✓																		
Total up	8		12		14		14		13		12		11		8		5		4		2		2		1		8	
Total down		10		11		14		14		13		12		11		8		5		4		2		2		1		8
Control group:																												
C-01	✓	✓					✓	✓																				
C-02	✓	✓					✓	✓																				
C-03		✓					✓	✓																				
C-04	✓	✓					✓	✓																				
C-05	✓	✓					✓	✓																				
C-06							✓	✓																				
C-07																												
C-08	✓	✓					✓	✓																				
C-09	✓	✓					✓	✓																				
C-10	✓	✓					✓	✓																				
C-11	✓	✓					✓	✓																				
C-12	✓	✓					✓	✓																				
C-13	✓	✓					✓	✓																				
C-14		✓					✓	✓																				
Total up	10						13																					
Total down		12						13																				

sions were classified as *belly crawling* if infants moved forward with their abdomens touching the ground and as *hands-and-knees crawling* if they traveled the entire length of the walkway with their abdomens off the surface. *Walking onset* was defined as the first day infants could travel 321 centimeters (the horizontal length of the extended walkway) without falling, holding a support, or pausing for longer than 3 seconds between steps.

Parents kept daily checklist diaries noting their infants' progress toward crawling and walking. To verify crawling and walking onset, a research assistant tracked parents' diary reports with weekly telephone interviews, and she conducted a lab visit or home visit (with walkway carpet in tow to measure distance). One infant (C-05) managed to travel long distances by rolling sideways, and one (E-15) hitched forward in a sitting position, but the assistant waited until each infant began moving in a prone position before counting their crawling onset day. Another infant (C-07) never crawled and instead proceeded directly to walking; accordingly, she did not contribute crawling data to this study.

There was a wide range in the ages at which children began crawling (4.8–9.6 months) and walking (9.3–14.9 months). Thus, age varied widely at each test session. Figure 3 shows the ages at which infants began crawling on their bellies (dotted bars), crawling on their hands and knees (filled bars), and walking (striped bars); the length of the bars represents duration of experience with each type of locomotion. Nine experimental-group infants and six control-group infants belly crawled before they began crawling on their hands and knees. (Infant E-12 also belly crawled for 6 days, but she crawled on her hands and knees at her first day of testing.) There were no differences in ages between experimental- and control-group infants in terms of when they began crawling on their bellies or on their hands and knees (all p's > .10). However, experimental-group infants were slightly older ($M = 12.6$ months) than controls ($M = 11.4$ months) when each group began walking ($t[26] = 2.23$, $p < .034$).

SLOPING WALKWAY AND STAIRS

Safe and risky slopes were created by adjusting the slant of a wooden walkway (Figure 4). The walkway had three sections connected by dowel hinges. Flat starting and landing platforms at each end of the walkway (83.6 centimeters wide × 76.8 centimeters long × 4.3 centimeters thick) flanked a sloping section in the middle (79.5 × 91.0 × 4.3 centimeters). One end section rested on a 71.0-centimeter-high stationary platform, so the total height was 75.3 centimeters. The other end rested on a modified hydraulic car jack. Cranking and releasing the jack raised and lowered the platform from 75.3 to 21.8 centimeters, causing the middle section of the walkway to

TABLE 2

CHILDREN CONTRIBUTING DATA TO UPHILL AND DOWNHILL TRIALS OVER WEEKS OF WALKING

CHILD'S NUMBER	WEEKS OF WALKING																			
	1st		4th		7th		10th		13th		16th		19th		22d		25th		28th	
	Up	Down	Up	Down	Up	Down	Up	Down	Up	Down	Up	Down	Up	Down	Up	Down	Up	Down	Up	Down
Experimental group:																				
E-01	✓	✓	✓	✓	✓	✓	✓	✓	✓	✓	✓	✓	✓	✓	✓	✓	✓	✓	✓	✓
E-02	✓	✓	✓	✓	✓	✓	✓	✓												
E-03	✓	✓	✓	✓	✓	✓	✓	✓												
E-04	✓	✓	✓	✓	✓	✓	✓	✓	✓	✓										
E-05	✓	✓	✓	✓	✓	✓	✓	✓												
E-06	✓	✓	✓	✓	✓	✓	✓	✓	✓	✓										
E-08	✓	✓	✓	✓	✓	✓	✓	✓	✓	✓	✓	✓	✓	✓						
E-09	✓	✓	✓	✓	✓	✓	✓	✓	✓	✓										
E-10	✓	✓	✓	✓	✓	✓	✓	✓												
E-11	✓	✓	✓	✓	✓	✓	✓	✓												
E-12	✓	✓	✓	✓	✓	✓	✓	✓	✓	✓	✓	✓			✓	✓				
E-13	✓	✓	✓	✓	✓	✓	✓	✓	✓	✓										
E-14	✓	✓	✓	✓	✓	✓	✓	✓												
E-15	✓	✓				✓														
E-16	✓	✓			✓	✓	✓	✓												
Total up	15		13		14		14		7		3		2		2		1		1	
Total down		15		13		15		14		7		3		2		2		1		1

Control group:

C-01	✓	
C-02	✓	
C-03		✓
C-04	✓	✓
C-05	✓	✓
C-06	✓ ✓	
C-07	✓ ✓	✓
C-08	✓ ✓	✓
C-09	✓ ✓	
C-10	✓ ✓	
C-11	✓ ✓	
C-12	✓ ✓	
C-13	✓ ✓	
C-14	✓ ✓	
Total up	12	1 1
Total down	12	1 1

41

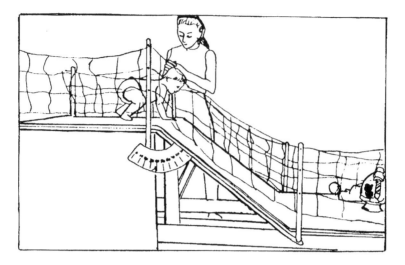

FIGURE 4.—Walkway with adjustable slope. Infants began at one flat end of the walkway and traversed the sloping middle section while an experimenter followed alongside to ensure their safety. Parents waited at the far end of the walkway and encouraged infants' efforts.

be flat or to slope in 2° increments from 0° to 36°.[1] Wooden posts at the corners of each platform provided the children with manual support, and a soft carpet provided traction and a cushion against falls. Safety nets stretched along both sides of the walkway.

An additional platform (83.6 centimeters wide × 76.8 centimeters long × 75.3 centimeters high) extended the horizontal length of the walkway from 244.5 to 321.3 centimeters for measuring walking proficiency on a flat surface. The carpet was removed and butcher paper rolled over the walkway for collecting footprint sequences. To assess transfer across different ascent and descent problems, infants were also tested on a single, carpeted stair of standard riser height (79.0 centimeters wide × 91.0 centimeters long × 15.2 centimeters high).

PROCEDURE

Each session included five series of tests to assess infants' progress on slopes and to describe the larger developmental context for change. First,

[1] Because a slope is a right triangle, changes in slant covary either with changes in the height of the hill or with changes in the length of the slope. In this experiment, the diagonal length of the slope remained constant, and the slant covaried with the vertical distance between the starting and the landing platforms (steeper slopes had a larger vertical drop-off). Although infants could use information about both the slant and the height of slopes, results of a previous control experiment showed that babies distinguish safe from risky slopes when

the experimenter verified items in parents' home diaries with tests of various *milestones* (sitting independently, pulling up to a stand, balancing, cruising upright while holding a handrail, moving from sitting to prone positions and vice versa, pivoting 180° prone, turning 180° in a sitting position, and taking independent walking steps). She also questioned parents about entries regarding falls and experience ascending and descending furniture, stairs, and playground slides. Second, babies went up and down the lab *stair*. Third, changes in babies' everyday *crawling and walking proficiency* were assessed on the flat walkway. Fourth, the bulk of the session involved testing on uphill and downhill *slopes*. Finally, the experimenter collected several measures of infants' *body dimensions*.

Typical test sessions lasted 120–135 minutes when infants first began crawling and walking and 90–105 minutes when they had become more expert. At their first sessions, several babies crawled so slowly or became so exhausted that uphill and downhill protocols were split over 2 consecutive days. When infants were crawlers, they wore only diapers during test sessions. After children began walking, they also wore rubber-soled shoes. An assistant videotaped milestone tests, stair climbing, and all trials on the flat walkway and slopes with the camera providing a sagittal view of the babies.

Slope Boundaries

The experimenter used a modified psychophysical staircase procedure (after Adolph, 1995) to identify uphill and downhill slope boundaries for each infant at each test session. Slope boundaries represented the steepest slopes infants could manage using their current, typical method of travel— crawling on their bellies, crawling on their hands and knees, or walking. By definition, hills shallower than slope boundary were safe for crawling or walking. Hills steeper than boundary were increasingly risky and required an alternative sliding or climbing method to reach the landing platform.

The staircase procedure is similar to Piaget's (1961) concentric clinical method: the size of the "steps" (the degree of slope) depends on children's performance on previous trials, and most trials are presented at increments where behavior is most variable (Gibson & Olum, 1960). A general rule of thumb is to present stimuli in increasing increments away from baseline until a change in response, then decreasing increments toward baseline until another change, and so on, until reaching a predetermined criterion (Cornsweet, 1962). In this study, infants received trials on increasingly steeper slopes until they either could not or would not use their typical locomotor

---

the height of the hills remains constant (Eppler et al., 1996). Toddlers walked down a long 10° slope but slid down a short 36° one.

method, then trials on shallower slopes until they again used their typical method successfully.

Infants began trials facing the slope from their typical vantage point. Crawlers began in their typical crawling position, and walkers began in their typical upright position. Parents stood at the far end of the walkway and encouraged their infants to come up or down, offering toys and Cheerios as enticements. An experimenter followed alongside infants to ensure their safety if they began to fall. The adults did not tell children what locomotor method to use; infants had to decide for themselves whether slopes were safe or risky for their typical method of locomotion. Trials began when infants looked toward the landing platform, and they lasted 60 seconds. If children did not start onto a hill within this time, or if they became extremely fussy, the experimenter ended the trial. Uphill and downhill trials were blocked. Half the infants went up hills first and half down first, at alternate sessions.

The experimenter scored each trial on-line as *success* with the infant's typical method (crawled or walked safely), *failure* (tried typical method but fell), or *refusal* to use his or her typical method (used alternative locomotor method or avoided going). For the purpose of identifying slope boundaries, the staircase procedure treated failures and refusals as equivalent outcomes. Because the staircase procedure focused only on infants' decisions relative to their typical locomotor method, attempts to use alternative locomotor methods were scored as refusals, regardless of success in the alternative position. Figure 5 illustrates a representative staircase protocol for a walking infant on downhill slopes.

As in previous research (Adolph, 1995), uphill trials began at easy 6° baselines and downhill trials at 4° baselines (a few children were so unsteady in their first week of walking that shallower 2° or 0° baselines were necessary). In general, the experimenter increased slant by 6° after each success and decreased slant by 4° after two consecutive unsuccessful trials. Failures and refusals were repeated at the same hill for reliability. Easy baseline trials followed negative outcomes on staircase trials (two failures or refusals) to renew infants' motivation to continue and to minimize trial order effects. As the experimenter narrowed in on infants' slope boundaries, she presented hills in smaller 2° increments. The series continued until children met a 67% criterion for establishing their slope boundaries: *the steepest hill where infants used their typical method at least two of three times successfully* and failed or refused at least two of three trials at the next 2° increment. If the experimenter was unsure about the outcome of a trial (noted by the question mark on trial 3 in Figure 5), she repeated it or continued the series until clearly meeting the 67% criterion. The 67% criterion minimized the total number of trials required while ensuring at least four to six trials directly at and around slope boundary. After identifying slope boundary, the experimenter presented infants with two trials on the 36° slope to see how they coped with the steepest increment.

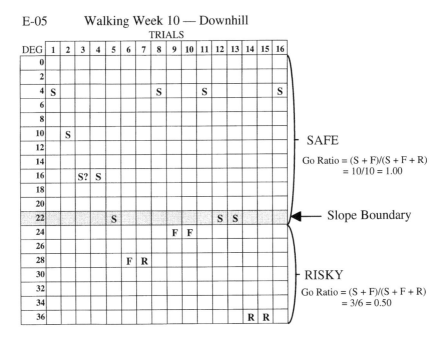

E-05   Walking Week 10 — Downhill

FIGURE 5.—Example of the psychophysical staircase procedure for one walking infant. Consecutive trials run across columns, and degrees run across rows. S = success with typical walking method (walked safely). F = failure (tried typical walking method but fell). R = refusal to walk (used alternative method of locomotion or avoided going). In general, steeper hills were presented after successful trials and shallower hills after failures or refusals until identifying infants' slope boundaries to a 67% criterion. Brackets to the right of the figure designate the distinction between safe hills shallower and including the boundary slope and risky hills steeper than the boundary slope. Go ratios were calculated according to the two-group method.

Owing to the personalized nature of the staircase procedure, children received trials at different increments of slope, and different numbers of trials were required to identify slope boundary. However, all children had multiple trials on baseline slopes and at 36°, and all had multiple trials at slope boundary and on hills slightly shallower and steeper than boundary (unless boundary was at 0° or 36°). The total number of trials per session ranged from seven (when slope boundary was at 36°) to 47 (when infants were particularly unruly or obstinate); the average was 15.28 uphill trials and 20.82 downhill trials per session. Across sessions and infants, there were 3,285 uphill trials and 4,559 downhill trials. The overall range for experimental-group infants was from 113 to 247 uphill trials and from 102 to 369 downhill trials. Control-group infants had far less practice on slopes. The range was from 25 to 53 uphill trials and from 30 to 81 downhill ones.

It is important to note that slope boundaries were conservative estimates of infants' physical ability on slopes because they represented only infants' demonstrated ability at each session; it is possible that infants could refuse or fail on perfectly safe hills owing to changes in their response criteria. However, other studies (Adolph, Gill, et al., 1996; Avolio, Thompson, Lin, Biswas, & Arnet, 1997) show strong test-retest reliability of the staircase procedure, and the practice of presenting baseline slopes after failures and refusals encouraged infants to demonstrate the upper limits of their physical prowess. In addition, the longitudinal design provides a ready check for the reliability of boundary estimates; that is, boundary should increase with weeks of crawling and walking experience.

Stair

Testing on the lab stair was a simplified version of the procedure for slopes. Crawling infants began each trial in a prone position, and walking infants started upright. Parents encouraged their babies to come up or down the stair, while an experimenter monitored infants to ensure their safety. Infants had two consecutive ascending and two consecutive descending trials.

Locomotor Proficiency on Flat Ground

Crawling data were collected on videotape. Infants crawled over the flat walkway four times, twice in each direction, ensuring that each side of their body was closest to the video camera for half the trials.

Walking data were collected from footprint sequences (Adolph, 1995; Adolph et al., 1993a). Babies wore inked moleskin tabs on the bottoms of their shoes at the toes and heels—triangular tabs at their toes and square tabs at their heels (see Figure 8a below). Infants walked over the flat, extended walkway, leaving behind a trail of footprints. Each walker contributed at least two sequences per session to verify the reliability of gait measures across consecutive trials.

Body Dimensions

At the end of each session, infants reclined on a changing table while the experimenter measured their head circumference (at eyebrows), recumbent height (crown to heel), leg length (anterior iliac spine to medial malleolus), and weight (on a pediatric scale). In addition, the Ponderal index (weight/height^3) provided a measure of infants' overall chubbiness (Shirley, 1931). All babies showed continuous growth for each variable, providing a crude indication that body measures were reliable.

V. DATA CODING

All slope data were scored from videotapes using a computerized coding system, MacSHAPA (Sanderson, McNeese, & Zaff, 1994; Sanderson, Scott, et al., 1994), that computes duration from frame numbers of onset and offset times, records categorical data and frequency counts, and provides precise, frame-by-frame, fingertip control of the VCR. Only video data were used for analyses.

SLOPE BOUNDARIES AND ADAPTIVE RESPONDING

A primary coder viewed each session and rescored trials as success, failure, or refusal. These data were used to recalculate slope boundaries to the 67% criterion (steepest slope with success on at least two of three trials) and to measure changes in the adaptiveness of infants' responses.

Go Ratios

A *go ratio* (Adolph, 1995) indexed the adaptiveness of infants' responses on safe and risky hills: number of attempts to go divided by total number of trials ([successes + failures] / [successes + failures + refusals]). Presumably, children would attempt their typical locomotor method if they perceived safe going and would select an alternative strategy if they perceived danger from falling. The go ratio was 1 if infants always attempted their typical method (successes and failures); the ratio was 0 if infants always selected an alternative strategy (refusals). The inverse *no-go ratio* ([refusals] / [successes + failures + refusals]) yields the same information.

Figure 6 illustrates the logic of this go ratio. Perfectly adapted responses would result in a go ratio curve that exactly matched the probability of success at each slope. Alternatively, infants could err on the side of boldness, indicated by a high go ratio on hills steeper than slope boundary, or err on the

$$\text{Go Ratio} = \frac{(S + F)}{(S + F + R)}$$

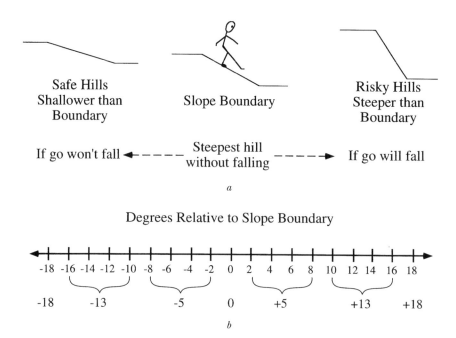

FIGURE 6.—a, Logic of the go ratio ([successes + failures]/[successes + failures + refusals]). Adaptive responding is indicated by a close correspondence between probability of success and the go ratio. b, Seven groups of slopes normalized to infants' slope boundaries.

side of caution, indicated by a low ratio on demonstrably safe hills shallower than boundary. Go ratios were 0.67 or higher at slope boundary by definition, but ratios could vary freely from 1 to 0 on hills steeper or shallower than boundary. Also by definition, success was rare on hills steeper than boundary, and go ratios therefore depended largely on the proportion of failures to refusals. This proportion was statistically independent from estimates of slope boundaries, which treated failures and refusals in the same way. Likewise, failures were rare on hills shallower than slope boundary, and go ratios therefore depended largely on the proportion of successes to refusals.

Like any measure of perceptual judgments, the go ratio may be affected by infants' response criteria (bias toward erring on the side of caution or the side of boldness). For example, a perfect step function, where go ratios drop to 0 on the first hill steeper than slope boundary, would indicate a conservative response criterion. However, the go ratio reflects an unbiased measure of the consistency of children's judgments within and across test sessions (Adolph, 1995). If children select locomotor methods relative to their current level of locomotor proficiency, then go ratios should be high on hills shallower than slope boundary and decrease continuously on each hill steeper than boundary. No relation between go ratios and degree of slope would indicate indiscriminate responding.

In principle, there is a go ratio for every slope. For example, in Figure 5 above, the baby had a go ratio of 1.0 at his 22° slope boundary, 1.0 at 24°, 0.5 at 28°, and so on. However, in practice, children received only one to three trials on most slopes, and children received trials on different slopes at each session. To compile more meaningful go ratios, and to facilitate statistical comparisons between children and across sessions, trials on successive slopes were grouped together, and go ratios were calculated for each group of slopes. The effect of grouping data across slopes for individual children was to create a more continuous index of infants' judgments and to smooth out chance irregularities, especially on hills close to slope boundary, where children received most trials.

Slope trials were grouped together in two ways. As shown on the right-hand side of Figure 5, the first technique clustered slopes into *two groups:* safe hills shallower than and including the boundary slope and risky hills steeper than slope boundary. This technique provided a clear, overall picture of change in the adaptiveness of infants' responses and was especially useful for comparing infants' judgments with weekly change in their exploratory activity. In addition, the two-group technique largely circumvented the problem of missing data in statistical comparisons because children always had trials on both safe and risky hills unless their slope boundaries were at 36°. The go ratio for risky hills primarily reflected infants' behavior on hills slightly steeper than slope boundary, where they received the largest proportion of trials. For example, the child in Figure 5 had a go ratio of 1.0 on safe hills and 0.50 on risky ones; the relatively high ratio on risky hills was due largely to failures on hills slightly steeper than boundary.

The second technique provided a more finely grained description of change. As in previous research (Adolph, 1995), slopes were clustered into *seven groups,* denoted by their midpoints: 0°, ±5°, ±13°, and ±18° (see Figure 6b). These groups correspond, respectively, to slope boundary, hills slightly shallower or steeper than the boundary, an intermediate range of hills, and hills considerably steeper or shallower than the boundary. The four groups surrounding slope boundary each spanned 8°, and the two most remote groups captured remaining trials on hills at least 18° shallower or steeper than the boundary. The size of the groups maximized the number of infants contributing data and the average number of trials per subject while preserving detail in the measurements. For example, returning to the data in Figure 5 above, the baby had three failures and one refusal in the +5° group of slopes spanning 24°–30°. The go ratio for +5° is 0.75, and ratios decreased from 1.0 at slope boundary to 0 at +13°. He had no trials at +18° because steeper hills were not available.

Despite the finer detail provided by the second technique, the seven groupings were affected more adversely by missing data. Children with low or moderate slope boundaries were often missing trials in the +13° range because, after identifying slope boundary, the experimenter skipped directly to the 36° hill. Children with very steep boundaries were missing data in the +13° and +18° ranges because these increments of slope were not available. The latter problem was most conspicuous in later weeks of crawling, when many infants' slope boundaries were near ceiling, providing data only in the +5° range, or slope boundaries were at 36°, providing no data on risky slopes. Thus, statistical comparisons relied on the two-group rather than the seven-group technique of combining slope trials.

LOCOMOTOR METHODS

A primary coder scored infants' locomotor methods for ascent and descent from videotapes of each test session. For trials scored as refusals, these data indicated whether infants switched from their typical locomotor method to a less perilous method of travel or simply avoided going onto the hill. The various climbing and sliding methods required infants to shift to a new position, but they had the benefit of greater stability, and the probability of falling on risky slopes was therefore lower. In contrast, avoidance required no physical effort and was, in principle, always available in infants' repertoires because it did not require them to master a new locomotor skill. On the other hand, avoidance was frustrating because babies had to wait out the entire trial despite parents' persuasive exhortations to come up or down. Most important, perfectly adapted go ratios required only two responses—infants' typical locomotor method plus one of the refusal methods. Use of more than two methods would indicate not only that infants treated some hills as safe and some as risky but also that infants used a variety of behavioral options at each session. In addition, these data portrayed the emergence of new locomotor methods in infants' repertoires.

As illustrated in Figure 7, there were three potential methods for coping with uphill trials: clambering up on four limbs, walking, and avoiding traversal. There were six potential methods for descent: crawling on hands and knees, walking, sliding headfirst prone, sliding in a sitting position, scooting down backward feet first, and avoiding traversal.

On uphill trials, prone and crawling methods were collapsed into a single

	clamber	walk	avoid
Belly Crawler	√		√
Hands-Knees Crawler	√		√
Walker	√	√	√

a

	crawl	walk	prone	sit	back	avoid
Belly Crawler			√	√	√	√
Hands-Knees Crawler	√		√	√	√	√
Walker	√	√	√	√	√	√

b

FIGURE 7.—Possible locomotor methods for going up and down hills for belly crawlers, hands-and-knees crawlers, and walkers. *a*, Uphill. *b*, Downhill.

quadruped, clambering category because it was not possible to distinguish deliberate shifts in quadruped positions from more serendipitous ones. Both belly crawlers and hands-and-knees crawlers pushed up onto their hands and knees or hands and feet after crossing the brink of the slope; on steeper hills, they exhibited a diffuse scrambling activity with all four limbs extended, almost standing upright as they tried vainly to make headway. Evidently, the upward hills pushed infants' weight over their legs; once their arms were partly relieved of supporting their body weight, even belly crawlers were able to extend their arms and balance on their hands and knees or hands and feet.

After infants began walking, they usually flung themselves forward onto upward hills with their feet and hands touching in quick succession. Occasionally, walkers approached upward hills more soberly by placing both hands on the slope in a quadruped position, putting one foot onto the hill before their hands, or taking a step or two onto the slope while holding a support post. The coders adopted a criterion of two feet on the hill before hands touched for scoring uphill trials as walking. No infant ever attempted a sitting or backing position on uphill slopes.

On downhill trials, all belly crawlers' attempts to go down headfirst were scored as their typical prone position. Hands-and-knees crawlers' attempts to go down headfirst were scored as their typical crawling method (crossing the brink on their hands and knees) or as an alternative prone sliding position (flattening out at the brink of the hills and slithering down spread-eagled and headfirst). Babies sometimes went down sideways with their bodies perpendicular to the length of the slope. This always occurred in the sessions when infants discovered the backing method. Sideways descents were counted as crawling if infants were facing down the hill toward the landing platform and as backing if they were facing away from the goal toward the starting platform.

All sitting (with both buttocks touching the surface) and kneeling positions were counted as sitting if infants' torsos were upright and babies were facing the landing platform regardless of whether both legs were extended in front or crumpled beneath the buttocks. In several cases, infants attempted to descend in a sitting position, facing away from the landing platform with their legs extended toward the top of the hill. The result was a backward somersault, and trials were scored as attempts to use the backing method. Walkers occasionally took one or two tiny steps onto a hill, sometimes holding a post for support, then stepped back onto the starting platform. Coders used a criterion of three forward steps over the brink without holding the posts for scoring descending trials as walking.

EXPLORATORY ACTIVITY

As in previous research (e.g., Adolph, 1995; Adolph et al., 1993a; Campos et al., 1978; Gibson et al., 1987), measures of children's exploratory activity on the starting platform were used to infer the informational basis of infants' decisions. Latency to start onto slopes provided a crude measure of visual exploration: very short latencies reflect quick glances, and long latencies reflect longer looking times. Frequency of touching slopes provided an index of haptic exploration: presumably, touching generates additional sources of information relevant to discriminating safe from risky slopes. Frequency of shifts in position provided a metric for means-ends exploration, shifts reflecting a search for an alternative locomotor method. Note, however, that, because coders used objective criteria to score infants' exploratory behaviors, coders could not distinguish between infants' intentional attempts to gather information and the same movements prompted by other factors (e.g., deliberate touching and touching prompted by fatigue were scored in the same way).

Each measure of exploratory activity was calculated independently from slope boundaries and go ratios. Exploration reflected infants' behavior *before* they started onto slopes, whereas slope boundaries and go ratios were determined by infants' behavior *after* they crossed the brink. In principle, refusals did not require prolonged exploration (e.g., infants could immediately choose an alternative method and slide down hills), and successes and failures did not prohibit prior exploration (e.g., infants could hesitate, touch hills, test various positions, then go heedlessly over the brink nonetheless).

Latency

A primary coder scored latency from all the sessions as time from the start of the trial until children began moving onto the slopes. Trials began when infants' bodies, heads, and eyes were oriented toward the landing platform, ensuring that infants made visual contact with the slope at the start of the trial. Time to get into position and approach the slope was subtracted so that latency reflected only hesitation rather than difficulty of switching from one position to another. This practice biased codes conservatively toward shorter latencies on downhill trials, where children required more time to change positions. If babies fussed or avoided going for the duration of the trial, coders scored latency as lasting 60 seconds or until the experimenter stopped the trial, whichever occurred first. If infants started onto slopes right away, the coder scored latency as 0.1 second. Walking infants often held onto a supporting post and stood at the edge of downhill slopes for several moments before starting down. The coder counted this period as hesitation until babies released their grip on the post. During the time infants hesitated, they looked at slopes, touched slopes, moved around on the starting platform, tested various locomotor positions, or engaged in evasive behaviors such as pulling at the safety nets, begging for toys, or beseeching the experimenter or their parents for help.

Touching

Principle codes for touching were frequency counts rather than duration because of the immense amount of data. A primary coder noted each trial where infants explored slopes by touching and whether babies held onto the supporting post during the touch. Touching included only active contact with slopes (Gibson, 1962), where infants stopped moving forward and oriented their head and body toward the landing platform. Touches included pressing, patting, and rubbing slopes with the hands or feet and rocking and small stepping movements of the hands or feet over the edge of the hill. Only hand touches were scored for crawlers, and both hand and foot touches were scored for walkers. Touches with the feet from a sitting position were not counted.

Shifts in Position: Means-Ends Exploration

Coders measured children's exploration of different locomotor methods by counting the number of discrete shifts in position before starting onto slopes. Refusals required no shifts to avoid traversal and only one shift for an alternative clambering or sliding position. Multiple shifts, therefore, would suggest that children explored various means of reaching the landing platform by testing what different positions felt like before committing themselves to going.

A primary coder scored shifts for all trials. The coder counted the following positions only if children held them for at least 0.5 second: standing, squatting, kneeling, sitting, crawling, lying prone with stomach down, and backing. In addition, the coder noted whether infants held a supporting post while shifting, whether they pivoted in a prone position, and whether they attempted to detour off the far edge of the starting platform, although these behaviors were not counted as separate shifts. For example, a walking infant's shifts from upright, to sitting, to standing, to prone would count as three shifts in position. Although there are fewer viable methods for going uphill, children sometimes explored nonviable alternatives (e.g., sitting) and sometimes tested the same position several times during a trial (e.g., alternating between crawling and sitting).

INTERRATER RELIABILITY FOR INFANTS' BEHAVIOR ON SLOPES

A second coder independently scored video data for each variable from one uphill and one downhill protocol from each infant, with sessions spread evenly across weeks of crawling and walking. Interrater reliability was high for each measure. Agreement for success, failure, and refusal across 1,033 trials was 96.72% for uphill sessions and 93.89% for downhill sessions. Agreement for type of locomotor method across 1,012 trials was 99.56% for uphill sessions and 99.82% for downhill sessions. Correlation coefficients between coders' judgments for latency over 1,012 trials were .99 for uphill trials and .97 for downhill trials. Agreement for touching over 991 trials was 99.32% for uphill and 92.41% for downhill. Agreement for each shift in position over 991 trials was 99.82% for ascent and 98.37% for descent; correlation coefficients for number of shifts were .98 for ascent and .99 for descent.

LOCOMOTOR PROFICIENCY ON FLAT GROUND

Changes in infants' crawling proficiency on flat ground were scored from videotapes. Changes in walking proficiency on flat ground were scored from footprint sequences.

Crawling

Videotapes of infants' four crawling trials on the flat walkway were viewed frame by frame. Coders identified the video frames where infants passed the second and third support posts. These landmarks denoted the middle 91-centimeter section of the walkway. This distance divided by total time for travel between the two posts yielded a measure of overall velocity. In addition, coders counted the number of crawling cycles (from offset to offset of the left hand) from one landmark post to another, excluding partially completed cycles at the beginning and end of each trial. Number of cycles provided a crude measure of step length (fewer cycles indicates larger movements). Improvements in crawling proficiency are associated with larger, faster movements (Freedland & Bertenthal, 1994; Vereijken et al., 1995).

A primary coder scored video data from each crawling session. A second coder independently scored timing data from the first trial from 51 randomly selected sessions, representing data from each child and 2,616 video frames altogether. For timing data, interrater reliability was 92.3% agreement within 2 video frames (0.07 second) and 95.6% agreement within 3 video frames (0.1 second). The second coder also scored number of cycles from the first two trials of 68 randomly selected sessions, representing data from each child and 441 cycles. Coders were in exact agreement on 97.8% of trials.

Walking

Footprint sequences yielded measures of children's walking proficiency on flat ground (Adolph, 1995; Adolph et al., 1993a; Adolph, Vereijken, et al., 1996). Only the middle section of each sequence—where children had hit their stride—was analyzed (Breniere et al., 1989). Coders identified the x and y coordinates of each square heel print and each triangular toe print using a transparent grid (0.1-inch units). A computer program transformed the coordinates into two primary measures of foot placement. As shown in Figure 8, measures were calculated relative to twists and turns in the path of progression. Step length is the distance between heel prints of alternate feet, and step width is the lateral distance between steps. Improvements in walking proficiency are associated with increased step length (e.g., Burnett & Johnson, 1971; Clark, Whitall, & Phillips, 1988) and decreased step width (e.g., Bril & Breniere, 1992a, 1992b; McGraw, 1945).

The computer program calculated mean values for each sequence and computed test-retest reliability of each measure across consecutive footprint

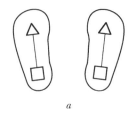

a

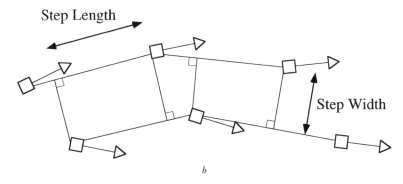

b

FIGURE 8.—Footprint measures of walking proficiency on flat ground. *a*, Triangular and square tabs placed at toes and heels on the bottoms of infants' shoes. *b*, Infants walked over butcher paper leaving behind a trail of footprints. Step length = distance between heel strikes of consecutive steps. Step width = lateral distance between feet. Both measures were calculated relative to twists and turns in the path.

sequences. Correlation coefficients indicated good reliability for both measures: step length (.85) and step width (.83). These values are comparable to those obtained from studies reporting footprint sequences of adults (e.g., Boening, 1977) and other studies with infants (Adolph, 1995; Adolph, Vereijken, et al., 1996).

VI. CHANGES IN INFANTS' ABILITY TO COPE WITH SLOPES

Infants' task was to decide how to go up and down safe and risky slopes. Adaptive responses required infants to select methods of locomotion on the basis of their current level of locomotor proficiency relative to the degree of slant. The first section below describes changes in infants' physical ability to go up and down slopes—their *slope boundaries*. The second section reports changes in the adaptiveness of infants' responses—their *go ratios* on safe and risky hills. The third section assesses change in infants' ability to obtain requisite information—their *exploratory activity*. The fourth section examines the emergence and variety of infants' *locomotor methods*. The final section examines *effects of practice* with slopes on all the preceding behaviors by comparing experimental-group infants with control-group infants.

Statistical analyses focused on five key sessions spanning the period of change (illustrated in Figure 2 above and Tables 1 and 2 above): infants' first and tenth weeks of crawling, their twenty-second week of crawling and beyond, and their first and tenth weeks of walking. Both experimental- and control-group infants contributed data to the first and tenth weeks of crawling and first week of walking. Note that figures showing group averages represent all infants contributing data to each session (the sample size is given in Tables 1 and 2). In contrast, in tables of statistical comparisons, sample size was reduced for paired *t* tests because fewer children contributed data to both comparison sessions. However, both ways of representing the data illustrate the same, general pattern of results.

SLOPE BOUNDARIES: CHANGES IN INFANTS' PHYSICAL ABILITY TO GO UP AND DOWN HILLS

Children's physical ability to go up and down hills changed at each test session with weeks of crawling and walking experience. Figure 9a shows changes in uphill and downhill slope boundaries for experimental-group infants (filled symbols) and control-group infants (open symbols) over weeks

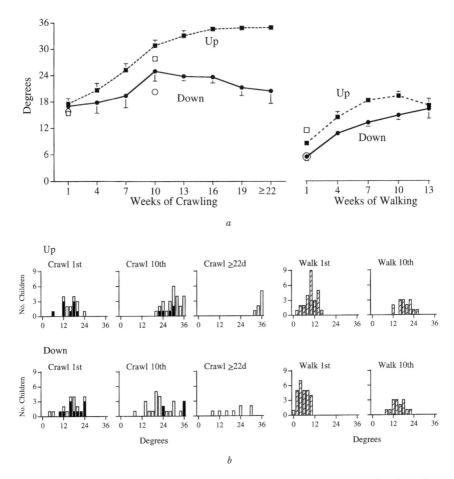

FIGURE 9.—a, Change in uphill and downhill slope boundaries over weeks of crawling and walking. Filled symbols = experimental-group infants. Open symbols = control-group infants. Bars denote standard errors. b, Frequency distributions of uphill and downhill slope boundaries at five key sessions. Bars represent both experimental- and control-group infants at the first and tenth weeks of crawling and the first week of walking. Only experimental-group infants are represented at the twenty-second week and beyond of crawling and the tenth week of walking. Solid bars = belly crawling. Open bars = hand-and-knees crawling. Striped bars = walking.

of crawling and walking. Figure 9b presents a more detailed view of the distributions of slope boundaries at five key test sessions. Sample size is larger at infants' first and tenth weeks of crawling and first week of walking, where both experimental- and control-group infants contributed data. Belly crawling is represented by solid bars, hands-and-knees crawling by open bars, and walking by striped bars.

Crawling boundaries depended on whether infants were going up or down and on the duration of infants' experience crawling on their bellies or on their hands and knees. In infants' *first* week of crawling, there was a wide range in slope boundaries (see the first column of Figure 9*b*). Belly crawlers (solid bars) had steeper boundaries on downhill slopes, and hands-and-knees crawlers (open bars) had steeper boundaries on uphill slopes. By the *tenth* week, most infants crawled on their hands and knees (see the second column of Figure 9*b*). The switch from belly to hands and knees facilitated improvement in uphill boundaries, where infants could take advantage of their leg strength. Determined belly crawlers attempted the steepest hills on trial after trial but fell back to the starting platform, leaving 10 long gouge marks in the carpet where they had dug in their fingers; hands-and-knees crawlers extended their arms and legs more fully and achieved the landing platform. In contrast, hands-and-knees crawlers had more trouble going downhill, where keeping balance is crucial. A few expert belly crawlers slid headfirst prone down the steepest 36° slope oblivious to balance requirements, but several new hands-and-knees crawlers showed a decrement in slope boundaries compared with their previous performance as belly crawlers. After 22 or more weeks of crawling, all infants moved firmly on their hands and knees. Each of these longtime crawlers had impressive uphill boundaries of 34° or 36° (see the third column of Figure 9*b*). However, on descending trials, there was still a large range in boundaries, and none of the infants crawled down the steepest hills.

Over the transition from crawling to walking, infants' slope boundaries sharply decreased (see Figure 9*a*). The decrement was dramatic and uniform. In their *first* week of walking, infants displayed a narrow range of slope boundaries limited to very shallow hills (see the fourth column of Figure 9*b*). Over weeks of walking, slope boundaries steadily increased. Infants managed an intermediate range of slopes by their *tenth* week of walking (see the fifth column of Figure 9*b*). Three infants tested at 19 or more weeks of walking (not shown in Figure 9) displayed impressive ability to walk up and down hills (28° was the steepest uphill boundary, and 36° was the steepest downhill boundary).

Statistical comparisons between progressive key sessions of experimental-group infants confirmed the steady increase in uphill and downhill slope boundaries over weeks of crawling and walking and the dramatic decrease over the transition from crawling to walking (see the top panel of Table 3). Although slope boundaries increased with weeks of experience, starting points were different for crawling and walking. Crawling over slopes was initially easier than walking over them. Statistical comparisons between crawling and walking boundaries matched for weeks of experience showed steeper boundaries for crawling than for walking in the first and tenth weeks of each method (see the bottom panel of Table 3).

TABLE 3

VALUE OF t OBTAINED IN COMPARISONS OF SLOPE BOUNDARIES OVER
PROGRESSIVE AND MATCHED TEST SESSIONS

	Up		Down	
	N	Paired t	N	Paired t
Progressive test sessions:				
Weeks of crawling:				
1st vs. 10th	7	−10.84***	9	−4.55**
10th vs. ≥22d	8	−3.06*	8	.74
Transition weeks:				
≥ 22d crawl vs. 1st walk	8	17.20***	8	5.13**
Weeks of walking:				
1st vs. 10th	14	−10.28***	14	−6.56***
Matched test sessions:				
Crawling vs. walking:				
1st week	8	5.27**	10	5.75***
10th week	13	5.55***	13	6.12***

NOTE.—Sample includes only experimental-group infants contributing data to both comparison sessions. Sample size varies because of missed test sessions and different amounts of crawling experience.

* $p < .05$.
** $p < .01$.
*** $p < .001$.

At most sessions, infants had steeper uphill slope boundaries than downhill (see Figure 9a). Statistical comparisons for experimental-group infants at key sessions showed steeper uphill boundaries than downhill at or beyond infants' twenty-second week of crawling, when all infants crawled on their hands and knees, and their first and tenth weeks of walking (see Table 4). The similarity between uphill and downhill crawling boundaries in infants' first and tenth weeks resulted from the asymmetrical consequences of belly crawling as opposed to crawling on hands and knees.

TABLE 4

VALUE OF t OBTAINED IN COMPARISONS OF UPHILL AND DOWNHILL
SLOPE BOUNDARIES AT KEY SESSIONS

	N	Paired t		N	Paired t
Weeks of crawling:			Weeks of walking:		
1st	8	.16	1st	15	3.72**
10th	14	2.11	10th	14	3.33**
≥ 22d	8	4.92**			

NOTE.—Sample includes only experimental-group infants contributing data to both uphill and downhill means. Sample size varies because of missed test sessions and different amounts of crawling experience.

** $p < .01$.

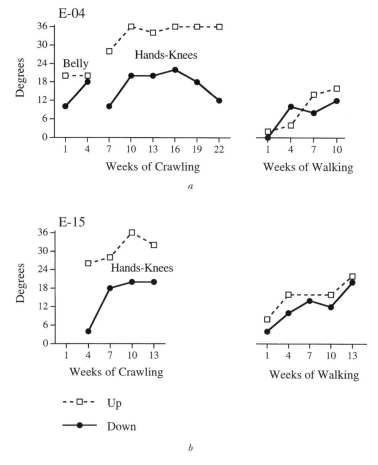

FIGURE 10.—Change in slope boundaries over weeks of crawling and walking for two experimental-group infants. *a*, E-04, who crawled on her belly and on her hands and knees prior to walking. *b*, E-15, who crawled only on her hands and knees.

Underestimation of Downhill Crawling Boundaries

Figure 10 illustrates changes in crawling boundaries observed in two experimental-group infants. E-15 crawled only on her hands and knees. Over her 13 weeks of crawling, uphill and downhill boundaries increased, and uphill boundaries were steeper than down. Over the transition from crawling to walking, boundaries decreased. Over weeks of walking, boundaries increased, and uphill boundaries were steeper than down. In contrast, E-04 crawled on her belly prior to crawling on her hands and knees, and she had 9 more weeks of crawling altogether. E-04 showed an asymmetrical decrease in her downhill crawling boundary (from 18° to 10°) over the transition from belly crawling to moving on her hands and knees but an increase in her uphill boundary (from 20° to 28°) at the same transition. Like E-15, infant E-04 showed a sharp decrease in boundaries over the transition from crawling to walking and an increase in boundaries over weeks of walking.

In addition, E-04's data illustrate a systematic underestimation in crawling boundaries. Inspection of boundaries across sessions shows that the staircase procedure underestimated E-04's downhill boundaries in her last week crawling on her hands and knees. At weeks 19–22, E-04's downhill boundaries decreased suddenly from 18° to 12°. This sudden decrease occurred because she refused to crawl down slopes she had managed successfully in previous weeks on her hands and knees.

Likewise, inspection of individual infants' slope boundaries across sessions showed systematic underestimation of downhill crawling boundaries in nine experimental-group infants. In each of these cases, crawling boundaries decreased suddenly relative to previous sessions, rather than increasing or asymptoting as expected. The drop in crawling boundaries was always greater than 4°, suggesting that the decrease was not due to random measurement error. Rather, infants staunchly refused to crawl down demonstrably safe hills that they had crawled down successfully in previous sessions. This systematic underestimation always occurred in expert, longtime crawlers' final session or two crawling on their hands and knees, and infants always replaced crawling on these steeper slopes with various sliding positions.

GO RATIOS: CHANGES IN ADAPTIVE RESPONDING

The primary measure of adaptive responding was infants' go ratios on safe and risky hills. In principle, the most adaptive responses would be evinced by low go ratios on risky hills and high ratios on safe ones, with continual updating in accordance with weekly changes in infants' slope boundaries. However, in practice, infants' go ratios may have been influenced by two additional considerations. First, infants may have taken into account the amount of effort and fun involved in executing various locomotor methods. For example, although crawling down steep slopes may have been possible, crawling may have been more effortful and less enjoyable than sliding down with a newfound sitting or backing method. In fact, in most cases where the experimenter underestimated infants' downhill crawling boundaries, infants insisted on using a new sitting or backing method on demonstrably safe slopes.

Second, infants were likely to consider the practical consequences of falling on downhill slopes compared with those of falling on uphill ones. Although the experimenter always rescued infants after they fell on downhill trials, falling while going downhill was clearly aversive. In contrast, on uphill trials, babies usually caught themselves after they fell, and the practical consequences were minimal. Infants were far more likely to fuss after falling on downhill trials than after falling on uphill ones. Previous cross-sectional experiments with crawling and walking infants indicated that infants take these different consequences into account by treating ascent and descent as very different tasks (e.g., Adolph, 1995; Adolph et al., 1993a).

Uphill Go Ratios

Uphill trials showed little evidence that infants distinguished safe from risky hills (see Figure 11*a*). In session after session, both for crawling and for walking, average go ratios of experimental-group (filled symbols) and control-group (open symbols) infants were close to 1.0 on safe and risky hills alike. When go ratios were calculated using the two-group safe/risky technique, on only three cases of the 215 protocols were infants' go ratios on risky slopes less than or equal to 0.50.

Likewise, a more detailed analysis of go ratios provided little evidence that infants discriminated safe from risky hills. Figure 12*a* shows experimental-group infants' go ratios calculated for the seven groups of slopes at key sessions. Thin lines and open symbols correspond to the four groups of safe slopes ($-18°$, $-13°$, $-5°$, and boundary), and thick lines and filled symbols correspond to the three groups of risky slopes ($+5°$, $+13°$, and $+18°$); all symbols represent data from three or more infants. As in the more global two-group analysis, uphill go ratios were high, near 1.0, at all slope increments except the impossibly steep $+18°$ range, where ratios were 0.63 and 0.45 in infants' first and tenth weeks of walking, respectively. Note, however, that many infants' crawling boundaries reached 36°, the steepest slope tested (43 protocols), with the result that risky hills were not available.

The prevalence of consistently high go ratios on risky uphill slopes could result only from a large preponderance of failures. This means that infants attempted hills on which they were likely to fall, despite falling on previous trials and in previous sessions. Infants often struggled to go up hills for the entire duration of the trial and, after such lengthy, frustrated attempts, tried equally hard moments later at the next trial on the same impossible slope. In many cases, persistence paid off, and infants eventually reached the summit. In the case of walkers, there was no practical reason for switching to an alternative crawling position before flinging themselves uphill. In fact, a running head start on two feet may be more sensible for biomechanical reasons because infants' center of mass exerts more frictional force when walking than when their weight is distributed over four limbs while crawling (Hudson & Johnson, 1976; Walker, 1989).

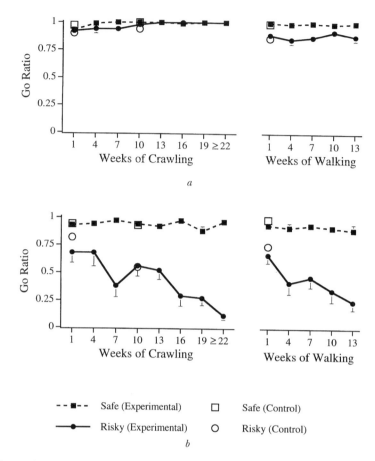

FIGURE 11.—Change in go ratios of experimental-group (filled symbols) and control-group (open symbols) infants over weeks of crawling and walking. Go ratio = ([successes + failures]/[successes + failures + refusals]). Trials are grouped into safe (dashed lines) and risky (solid lines) hills relative to infants' slope boundaries. Error bars represent standard errors. *a*, Uphill. *b*, Downhill.

Downhill Go Ratios

Although the consequences of falling while going uphill were minimal, falling while going downhill was more aversive, necessitating that infants be more discerning. Similar to the results on uphill trials, go ratios were uniformly high on *safe* downhill slopes (see Figure 11*b* above) for experimental-group (filled symbols) and control-group (open symbols) infants. Not surprisingly, when go ratios were calculated according to the two-group safe/risky method, there was not a single experimental- or control-group infant whose go ratios on safe hills dropped below 0.50 for either crawling or walking.

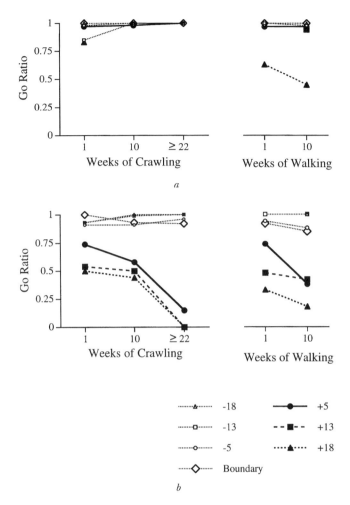

FIGURE 12.—Change in go ratios of experimental-group infants. Trials are averaged within seven groups of slopes denoted by their midpoints and calculated relative to infants' slope boundaries ($-18°$, $-13°$, $-5°$, 0, $+5°$, $+13°$, $+18°$). *a,* Uphill. *b,* Downhill.

However, in contrast to the results on uphill protocols, go ratios showed important changes on *risky* downhill slopes (see Figure 11*b*). In their first week of crawling, most infants plunged headlong down impossibly steep hills, and average go ratios were 0.68. Despite changes in infants' slope boundaries, over weeks of crawling, go ratios decreased steadily until, by the last week of crawling, infants' judgments were nearly perfect; average go ratios were 0.11 over the entire range of risky slopes.

Most striking, go ratios showed no transfer from crawling to walking. In

TABLE 5

VALUE OF *t* OBTAINED IN COMPARISONS OF GO RATIOS ON RISKY DOWNHILL SLOPES OVER
PROGRESSIVE AND MATCHED SESSIONS

	N	Paired *t*		N	Paired *t*
Progressive test sessions:			Progressive test sessions:		
Weeks of crawling:			Weeks of walking:		
1st vs. 10th	7	1.58	1st vs. 10th	14	4.51***
10th vs. 22d	6	4.03*	Matched test sessions:		
Transition weeks:			Crawling vs. walking:		
≥ 22d crawl vs. 1st walk ...	8	−5.37**	1st week	10	.55
			10th week	10	2.19

NOTE.—Sample includes only experimental-group infants contributing data to both comparison sessions. Sample size
varies because of missed test sessions and different amounts of crawling experience.
* $p < .05$.
** $p < .01$.
*** $p < .001$.

their first week of walking, infants walked over the edge of risky hills; average
go ratios were as high as in infants' first week of crawling (0.65). Over weeks
of walking, go ratios steadily decreased as infants began, all over again, to
adapt their current method of locomotion to the slope of the supporting
surface. By their thirteenth week of walking, average go ratios decreased to
0.24.

Statistical comparisons between progressive sessions of experimental-
group infants confirmed the steady decrease in go ratios on risky downhill
slopes over weeks of crawling and walking and the dramatic increase in go
ratios over the transition from crawling to walking. Table 5 shows mean values
and results of paired *t* tests for progressive and matched test sessions. Infants'
failure to transfer from crawling to walking was virtually complete. Comparisons between matched crawling and walking sessions showed no differences in go ratios, suggesting that learning was no faster the second time
around.

Safe and Risky Slopes

Although infants' errors were high in their first weeks of crawling and
walking, babies did show evidence of discriminating safe from risky downhill
slopes from the start. Paired comparisons revealed differences in go ratios
on safe and risky hills at each of the experimental-group infants' five key
sessions (see Table 6). The differences were due largely to the influence of
very easy baseline and shallow hills in the safe group of trials because errors
on risky hills were either uniformly high or low, especially over weeks of
crawling.

TABLE 6

VALUE OF t OBTAINED IN COMPARISONS OF GO RATIOS ON SAFE AND
RISKY DOWNHILL SLOPES AT KEY SESSIONS

	N	Paired t		N	Paired t
Weeks of crawling:			Weeks of walking:		
1st	10	3.06*	1st	15	5.43***
10th	11	4.49**	10th	14	6.29***
≥ 22d	8	25.13***			

NOTE.—Sample includes only experimental-group infants contributing data to both safe and risky slopes. Sample size varies because of missed test sessions, ceiling effects, and different amounts of crawling experience.
  * $p < .05$.
  ** $p < .01$.
  *** $p < .001$.

Consistency of Infants' Judgments

Figure 12*b* provides a more detailed portrayal of change in experimental-group infants' go ratios within and across key test sessions (each symbol represents data from three or more infants). *Across* sessions, go ratios decreased at each of the three groups of risky slopes (thick lines and filled symbols represent go ratios at +5°, +13°, and +18°). *Within* sessions, go ratios show strong consistency in infants' judgments. At each session, go ratios were scaled to infants' physical ability on slopes. Infants made the most errors on hills closest to their slope boundaries and the fewest errors on the steepest hills most remote from their boundaries. Go ratios for the four groups of safe slopes (−18°, −13°, -5°, and 0°) lie above curves for +5°, curves for +5° lie on or above those for +13°, and curves for +13° lie on or above those for +18°.

Individual protocols of experimental- and control-group infants make this point more salient. In 63% of the 219 downhill protocols, children's seven slope groups showed complete consistency. Each of the seven slope groups had constant or steadily decreasing go ratios, ordered from −18° to +18°. Ignoring the occasional blips where infants were overly cautious on safe hills, in 89% of protocols each of the slope groups had constant or steadily decreasing go ratios, ordered from boundary to +18°.

Specificity of Learning over Changes in Vantage Point

The early indication of infants' failure to transfer over the transition from crawling to walking inspired an additional experimental manipulation. After observing the first few seemingly knowledgeable crawling infants walk blithely over the brink of impossible hills the next week as new walkers, the experimenter added four extra trials at 36° to the end of walkers' downhill protocols. Infants received two 36° trials beginning in a standing position as usual, then two additional trials beginning in their old, familiar crawling position, then two more additional trials beginning once again in a standing position. The purpose of these additional trials was to examine the effects of changing vantage point on infants' responses. In addition, the six consecutive trials provided an opportunity to examine transfer from trial to trial.

All 15 experimental-group infants had additional trials at 36° during one or more walking sessions (11 babies had extra 36° trials in their first week of walking). Ten control-group infants had extra 36° trials in their first week of walking. These extra trials (240 in total) were analyzed separately and were not included in calculations of go ratios, exploratory activity, locomotor methods, or the total trial count for the experiment reported above.

Manipulation of walkers' starting position yielded three surprising results (Adolph & Pursifull, 1993). First, when started in their old, familiar, prone position, many children stood themselves up, preferring to face the hill as novice walkers rather than experienced crawlers. Ten experimental-group infants and seven control-group infants stood up from prone. Overall, children stood themselves up on 46 of 133 prone trials. On 43 trials where this occurred, infants stood up immediately, without hesitating, touching slopes, or shifting to other positions. After standing themselves up, infants did exactly what they did on trials where the experimenter started them in a standing position (see Figure 13). More discerning infants stood up, explored the slope, then selected an appropriate sliding position for descent. More hapless infants stood themselves up and walked over the edge with no hint of their prior crawling knowledge. Go ratios at 36° were similar regardless of whether the experimenter started children in a standing position ($M = .30$) or infants stood themselves up from a prone position ($M = .38$; $t[17] = 0.50$, $p > .10$).

Second, on prone trials when infants did not stand up, they behaved like their old crawling selves. As shown in the leftmost bars in Figure 13, experimental-group infants' go ratios on trials where they stayed prone ($M = 0.05$) were similar to go ratios at 36° in their final week of crawling ($M = 0.07$). Finally, adaptive responding sometimes failed to transfer over consecutive trials, even with a spur to remind infants that 36° was a risky slope. In these cases, walkers slid smoothly down the 36° hill when they were started and stayed in a prone position. However, in their very next trial, nine adaptive ex-crawlers attempted to walk down 36° when starting from a standing position.

Within-Session Learning

Just as consecutive trials at 36° did not teach infants how to make adaptive decisions about descent, there was no evidence of within-session learning over consecutive trials at other degrees of slope. The strongest evidence for

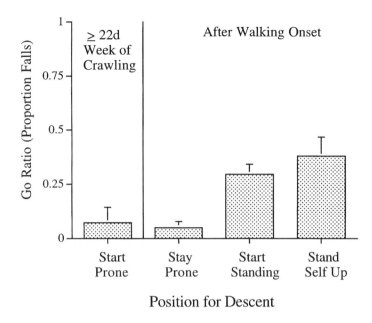

FIGURE 13.—Go ratios of experimental- and control-group infants at 36° in the last week of crawling and after they began walking. Bars reflect whether the infants began in a prone or in a standing position and whether the experimenter started the infants in a standing position or the infants stood themselves up.

within-session learning over consecutive trials would be if failures on one trial prompted refusals on the very next trial, on the very same slope (e.g., if falling at 20° prompted a refusal moments later at 20°). However, results showed the opposite effect. After failures, infants were most likely to persist with the same hapless response on consecutive trials at the same slope (this response occurred on 80% of trials); in other words, after children fell, they attempted the same crawling or walking method at the same slope moments later. In fact, successes on shallower hills (which occurred on 93% of trials), rather than failures, were most likely to precede refusals; that is, infants refused the steeper hills outright.

Summary: Slope Boundaries and Go Ratios

In sum, slope boundaries showed change in infants' physical ability to cope with slopes, and go ratios showed change in the adaptiveness of infants' responding on safe and risky downhill slopes. Most striking were the improvements in downhill go ratios over changes in infants' crawling and walking proficiency and infants' failure to transfer over the transition from crawling to walking. The evidence suggests that infants became increasingly adept at adapting their current method of locomotion to the properties of the supporting surface by judging degree of slant relative to their own level of locomotor proficiency. The next section examines the informational basis of infants' decisions, that is, sources of information pertinent to discriminating safe from risky hills.

EXPLORATORY ACTIVITY: CHANGES IN LATENCY AND TOUCHING

As in previous research (e.g., Adolph, 1995; Adolph et al., 1993a; Gibson et al., 1987), measures of infants' exploratory looking and touching were used to infer the informational basis of adaptive responses. The experimental procedure ensured that infants always had at least a quick glance at the slopes at the start of each trial. *Latency* to start onto slopes provided a crude measure of more extended visual exploration and visual/proprioceptive exploration as infants swayed back and forth on the starting platform. Frequency of *touching* slopes provided a crude measure of haptic exploration. Latency and touching were related measures because latency included the time that infants spent touching; correlation coefficients for each experimental- and control-group infant over weeks of crawling and walking up and down hills ranged from .35 to .87 ($M = .58$).

Uphill Exploration

Prolonged exploration before starting uphill was rare and indiscriminate. On most trials, infants started up hills after only a momentary glance. This means that infants' judgments about ascent were based primarily on visual information obtained in the moments during which the experimenter lowered them toward the starting platform and released them to begin the trial. As shown in Figure 14a, exploration prior to ascent was limited primarily to the first four weeks of crawling for both experimental-group (filled symbols) and control-group (open symbols) infants. However, in these sessions, infants hesitated and touched safe and risky hills indiscriminately. Paired comparisons between the latencies on safe and risky hills of experimental-group infants showed no differences at either the first or the fourth week of crawling (all p's $> .10$). Likewise, there were no differences between the proportions of touch trials on safe and risky hills in either the first or the fourth week of crawling (all p's $> .10$). In subsequent weeks of crawling and walking, infants flung themselves forward onto hills nearly as soon as the experimenter placed them on the starting platform.

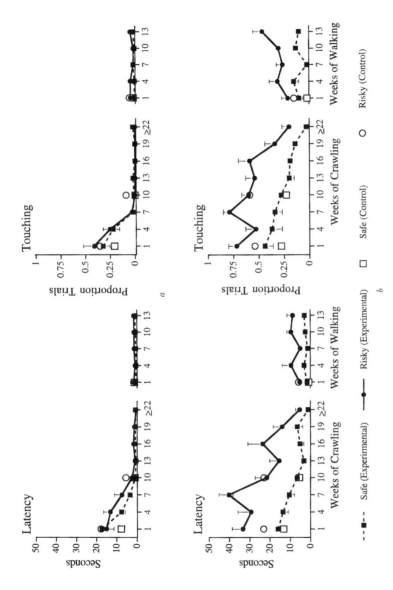

FIGURE 14.—Latency and touching of experimental-group (filled symbols) and control-group (open symbols) infants. Trials are grouped into safe (dashed lines) and risky (solid lines) hills relative to infants' slope boundaries. Error bars represent standard errors. *a*, Up-hill. *b*, Downhill.

Safe (Experimental) □   Safe (Control) □   Risky (Experimental) ■   Risky (Control) ○

- - - ■ - - - Risky (Experimental) ●

Weeks of Crawling   Weeks of Walking   Weeks of Crawling   Weeks of Walking

Latency   Touching

Seconds   Proportion Trials

Functional Outcome of Uphill Exploration

Despite hesitating and touching in their first 4 weeks of crawling, infants gained no immediate benefits from their exploratory activity. Go ratios at the first two crawling sessions were uniformly high at all seven safe and risky groups of slopes (see Figure 12*a* above). Conversely, there was virtually no hesitation or touching after babies began walking, although go ratios hovered around 0.50 at the steepest (+18°) group of slopes. Apparently, infants' judgments about going up hills were based on information obtained from a quick glance at the start of the trial, and this information was sufficient for making some adaptive judgments at the steepest slopes. Previous cross-sectional experiments showed similar results for exploration and go ratios during ascent in crawling and walking infants (Adolph, 1995; Adolph et al., 1993a).

Downhill Exploration

Downhill exploration showed two important changes. First, prolonged looking and touching decreased, with the result that infants' decisions were based increasingly on only a quick glance at the hill at the start of the trial. Second, exploratory movements became increasingly efficient, meaning that infants gleaned more from their exploratory movements, and locomotor decisions became more adaptive. Each of these changes is described below.

In contrast to uphill trials, infants engaged in more prolonged exploration prior to descent. Downhill exploration was more discriminating than uphill exploration from the start of crawling, and prolonged exploration decreased with weeks of locomotor experience. Similar to those obtained from ascent, measures of latency and touching during descent were highest in infants' first weeks of crawling. As shown in Figure 14*b*, over weeks of crawling, downhill exploration of experimental-group (filled symbols) and control-group (open symbols) infants gradually decreased, and infants' decisions about whether to go were therefore increasingly based on information obtained from only a quick glance as the experimenter released them at the start of the trial. There was no change from low levels of exploration over the transition from crawling to walking. Over weeks of walking, exploration began to increase, especially on risky slopes. In general, statistical analyses supported these trends, despite high variability and reduced sample size in comparisons between progressive test sessions (see the top panel of Table 7).

As in previous research (Adolph et al., 1993a), crawlers explored more than walkers. Comparisons between matched crawling and walking sessions of experimental-group infants showed higher levels of exploration in weeks of crawling (see the bottom panel of Table 7). The difference between crawlers' initially longer latencies and more frequent touches and walkers' shorter

TABLE 7

VALUE OF t OBTAINED IN COMPARISONS OF LATENCY AND TOUCHING ON SAFE AND RISKY DOWNHILL
SLOPES OVER PROGRESSIVE AND MATCHED SESSIONS

| | SAFE | | | RISKY | | |
| | | Paired t | | | Paired t | |
	N	Latency	Touching	N	Latency	Touching
Progressive test sessions:						
Weeks of crawling:						
1st vs. 10th	9	2.38*	1.30	7	.15	.86
10th vs. ≥ 22d	8	2.44*	3.51**	6	2.15	2.66*
Transition weeks:						
≥ 22d crawl vs. 1st walk	8	−1.24	−1.26	8	−.66	−.44
Weeks of walking:						
1st vs. 10th	14	−1.25	−.51	14	−3.56**	−3.05**
Matched test sessions:						
Crawling vs. walking:						
1st week	10	4.51**	4.12***	10	6.19***	7.23***
10th week	13	1.98	2.27*	10	2.89*	3.89**

NOTE.—Sample includes only experimental-group infants contributing data to both safe and risky slopes in both comparison sessions. Sample size varies because of missed test sessions, ceiling effects, and different amounts of crawling experience.

* $p < .05$.
** $p < .01$.
*** $p < .001$.

latencies and less frequent touches may result from the different biomechanical constraints of moving in quadruped and upright positions. For example, it may be more difficult for walking infants to execute exploratory procedures while attending to the immediate problem of maintaining upright balance. After walking onset, eight experimental-group infants held the corner posts while touching hills with their feet, as though requiring additional support to keep their balance (this occurred on 22% of 333 experimental-group infants' downhill touch trials). Only one crawler on only one trial held a post for support.

Although prolonged looking and exploratory touching decreased *across* sessions, infants showed signs of differential exploration from the start. *Within* sessions, infants hesitated and touched more on risky slopes than safe ones, especially during the first 10 weeks of crawling and when walking (see Table 8).

Functional Outcome of Downhill Exploration

Apparently, infants' exploratory movements became increasingly efficient. The functional outcome of downhill exploration improved with weeks of crawling and walking experience, marked by increasingly adaptive re-

TABLE 8

VALUE OF t OBTAINED IN COMPARISONS OF TOUCHING AND LATENCY ON SAFE AND RISKY
DOWNHILL SLOPES AT KEY SESSIONS

		PAIRED t				PAIRED t	
	N	Latency	Touch		N	Latency	Touch
Weeks of crawl-ing:				Weeks of walk-ing:			
1st	10	−3.41**	−3.24*	1st	15	−2.92*	−1.71
10th	11	−3.44**	−5.08***	10th	14	−4.31***	−3.66**
≥ 22d	8	−2.15	−2.09				

NOTE.—Sample includes only experimental-group infants contributing data to both safe and risky slopes. Sample size varies because of missed test sessions, ceiling effects, and different amounts of crawling experience.

* $p < .05$.
** $p < .01$.
*** $p < .001$.

sponses. As prolonged looking and touching decreased, exploratory activity also became more efficient. That is, infants actually explored less as their responses became more adaptive. Across sessions, infants' latency, touching, and go ratios changed in tandem. Latency and touching on risky hills paralleled infants' go ratios over weeks of crawling (cf. the graphs in Figure 11 above with those in Figure 14). All three measures showed increasing specificity as values geared in toward risky hills. In infants' first weeks of crawling, exploration was highest on both safe and risky hills, and infants' responses were least adaptive (risky go ratios were highest). In infants' final weeks of crawling, latency and touching were lowest and concentrated only on risky hills, and go ratios showed the most adaptive responses. Short latencies and infrequent touches in infants' last weeks of crawling and first weeks of walking meant that they relied increasingly on visual information obtained from a quick glance and step or two at the start of the trial to determine the risk of falling.

Figure 15 represents changes in the functional outcome of experimental-group infants' downhill exploration on risky slopes after three types of exploration: trials where infants took only a brief glance at the slope, trials where infants engaged in prolonged looking, and trials where infants hesitated and touched slopes. Here, functional outcome is portrayed as average go ratios on risky slopes (adaptive responses are indicated by low go ratios). Figure 15a shows the outcome of trials where infants took only a quick glance as they were lowered toward the starting platform and took a step or two at the start of the trial (latency ≤ 1 second, no touches). Figure 15b shows trials where babies stopped moving forward and took longer looks at the slope (latency > 1 second, no touches). Presumably, prolonged looking was accompanied by the gathering of proprioceptive information as infants swayed back

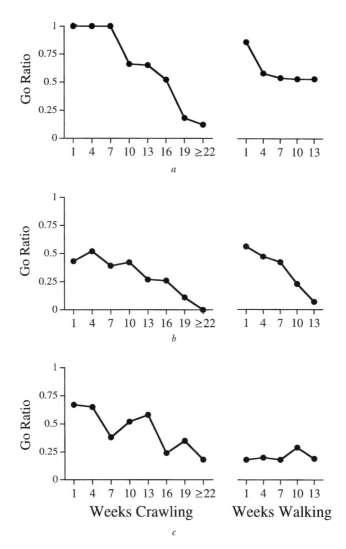

FIGURE 15.—Functional outcome (average go ratio) of experimental-group infants' exploratory looking and touching on risky downhill slopes over weeks of crawling and walking. *a*, Quick glances (latency ≤ 1 second, no touches). *b*, Long looks (latency > 1 second, no touches). *c*, Coordinated touching and looking.

and forth in a stationary position. Figure 15*c* shows trials where infants explored slopes by touching them.

Risky go ratios after both quick glances and prolonged visual/proprioceptive exploration showed two curves, one over weeks of crawling and the other over weeks of walking, with a sharp increase in errors over the transition from crawling to walking. Risky go ratios after touching showed improvement over weeks of crawling and a flat curve hovering around a 20% error rate over weeks of walking. Together, Figures 14 and 15 suggest that, over weeks of locomotor experience, briefer glances replaced prolonged looking and touching and that infants were able to glean more from their exploratory movements, enabling locomotor responses to become more adaptive.

A Closer Look at Touching

As described above, coders scored the overall data set only for the presence or absence of touching on each trial because of the large number of trials and the difficulty of coding duration and type of touching. However, more detailed measures of touching movements provide firmer evidence about the informational basis of infants' locomotor decisions.

To obtain a more finely grained description of touching, two coders together scored trials from selected sessions of four infants in a second pass through the data (infants E-03, E-04, E-08, and E-13 at their first and final weeks of crawling, an intermediate week of crawling, and their first and tenth weeks of walking). Overall, coders scored a total of 109 touches on downhill slopes. Coders identified the *duration* of each touch (from initial to final contact), the number of *limbs* used for touching (one hand/foot, both hands/feet), and two types of touching movements: pats/pokes/rubs (brief, continuously moving contacts with the surface) and rocking/stepping movements at the brink of the slope (infants' shoulders or hips rotating over their wrists or ankles). Presumably, pats/pokes/rubs provide less information that is relevant to balance control because they do not involve weight bearing; such movements may yield primarily information about slant and texture. Conversely, rocking/stepping movements may provide more information relevant to balance control because they involve weight bearing, generate torque and shearing forces at infants' wrists or ankles, and may simulate crawling and walking down slopes more closely.

There was a wide range in duration and number of touches across infants and sessions. Overall, the length of single touches ranged from 0.1 second to 51.53 seconds ($M = 7.64$ seconds). The duration of touches tended to decrease over weeks of crawling and remain low over weeks of walking. Most touches (78%) involved the use of both hands or both feet. Nearly all long touches were two limbed (94% of touches lasting 5 seconds or longer); more short touches were one limbed (33% of touches shorter than 5 seconds). Usually, infants stopped and looked at slopes for several seconds prior to their first touch, suggesting that visual information prompted the touch; average latency before infants' first touch was 6.08 seconds (range = 0–45.10 seconds), and 83% of first touches had latencies longer than 1 second.

Infants' preferred method of touching was rocking/stepping movements, although they sometimes touched in bouts, alternating between pats/rubs/pokes and rocking/stepping in a single, continuous touch. Most touches (52%) involved only rocking/stepping movements, 16% involved only pats/rubs/pokes, and 32% involved both types of touches in bouts. Rocking/stepping movements were most nerve-racking to observe because infants balanced right at the brink of the hills and their bodies sometimes rotated more than 90° over their supporting limbs. In contrast, pats/rubs/pokes were performed with crawlers' knees and walkers' supporting leg on the starting platform while the moving limb probed the slope ahead.

Control for Trial Order Effects

Infants received trials at easy baseline slopes (6° for up and 4° for down) interspersed with staircase trials to maintain their interest in the task and to control for order effects due to presenting several similar slopes on consecutive trials. Increase in latency on baseline trials would suggest that infants became tired or bored over the lengthy sessions. However, results showed no correlation between trial number and latency for crawling or walking uphill or down in experimental- or control-group infants; the average correlation coefficient was .04. Infants clearly enjoyed the slope task, and parents' enthusiasm helped sustain babies' interest over the many weeks of testing.

Summary: Latency and Touching

Overall, crawlers explored more than walkers, but latency and touching became increasingly selective over weeks of crawling and walking until prolonged exploratory activity was restricted primarily to downhill risky slopes. At the same time, the functional outcome of quick glances, long looks, and touches became increasingly adaptive, suggesting that exploratory movements became both more selective and more efficient. After determining whether hills were safe or risky, infants were still left with the problem of deciding how to go up or down. The next section examines the variety and emergence of infants' locomotor methods for tackling safe and risky slopes.

VARIETY IN LOCOMOTOR METHODS AND THE EMERGENCE OF NEW LOCOMOTOR PATTERNS

A key aspect of adaptive locomotion is flexible variety of means, rather than rigid adherence to a fixed solution. In the slope task, adaptive selection among various locomotor methods depended on the range of options available in infants' repertoires and the different benefits and drawbacks of each method. In general, trials on risky downhill slopes provided the clearest arena for examining variety in infants' locomotor methods. These trials required infants to determine the trade-off between using their typical method and selecting a viable alternative.

Uphill Methods

On uphill trials, infants nearly always attempted their typical locomotor method—crawlers went up hills crawling, and walkers went up walking. Figure 16a shows the average proportion of trials for each possible method on safe and risky hills over weeks of crawling and walking for experimental-group infants. Infants' typical locomotor method was virtually uniform on both safe and risky hills (filled squares for crawling and filled circles for walking). Note that the curves for infants' typical methods are identical to infants' go ratio curves in Figure 11 above. The additional information in Figure 16 is provided by the relative proportions of alternative methods used on refusal trials.

As in previous experiments (Adolph, 1995; Adolph et al., 1993a), avoidance was extremely rare on uphill trials. Infants in both the experimental and the control groups attempted any available method for ascent, rather than remain on the starting platform. Children avoided ascent on only 2% of trials over weeks of crawling and only 0.01% of trials over weeks of walking. Ten experimental-group infants initiated a tricky form of avoidance. Prior to starting uphill, they detoured off the starting platform and crawled or walked around the apparatus toward their parents at the far side. These tricky detours were limited to trials on steep slopes (when the starting platform was near the floor) and always occurred after very short latencies. In a few cases, frustrated infants detoured off the starting platform and ran straight out of the room.

Downhill Methods

Variety of Locomotor Methods

On downhill trials, where more potential options were available, infants used a larger variety of locomotor methods. Figure 16b shows the average proportion of each method used on safe and risky slopes. On *safe* hills, babies relied on their typical locomotor methods. In general, belly crawlers went down safe slopes prone (open squares), hands-and-knees crawlers went down on four limbs (filled squares), and walkers went down upright (filled circles). In contrast, *risky* downhill slopes elicited a medley of locomotor methods at each week of crawling and walking: crawling, sliding prone, and avoiding in

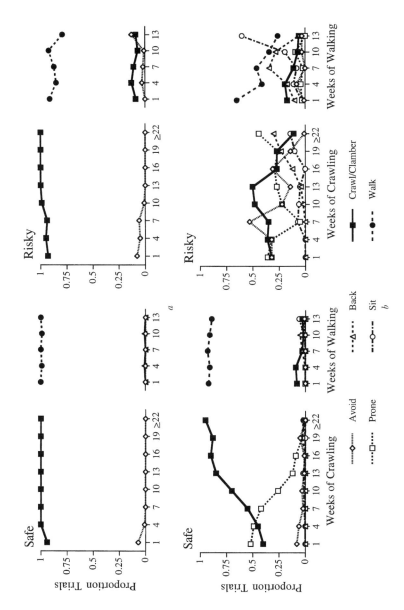

FIGURE 16.—Variety in locomotor methods on safe and risky hills. Curves represent average proportion of trials. Three responses were possible for uphill trials (clambering, walking, and avoiding), and six responses were possible for downhill trials (crawling, walking, sliding prone, sitting, backing, and avoiding). *a*, Uphill. *b*, Downhill.

TABLE 9

NUMBER OF EXPERIMENTAL-GROUP INFANTS USING VARIOUS NUMBERS OF
LOCOMOTOR METHODS FOR DESCENDING SAFE AND RISKY HILLS

| | NUMBER OF DESCENT METHODS | | | | | |
HILLS	1	2	3	4	5	6
Safe	0	0	2	4	5	4
Risky	0	1	0	0	4	10

infants' first weeks of crawling; additional sitting and backing positions in their last weeks of crawling; and all the sliding methods over weeks of walking.

Across sessions, most experimental-group infants used each of the six descent methods at least once (15 subjects crawled, 15 walked, 13 slid prone, 14 slid sitting, 14 slid backing, and 14 avoided). However, variety in infants' locomotor methods was restricted primarily to risky slopes. Ten experimental-group infants used all six methods to go down risky slopes, and four additional infants used five of the six methods (see Table 9). More infants used multiple methods on risky hills than on safe ones ($\chi^2[5] = 12.34$, $p < .05$).

Moreover, *within* sessions, individual infants used a variety of methods on risky slopes, indicating flexible means to achieve functional outcome. The average number of methods per session ranged from 1.80 to 2.00 in experimental-group infants' first through tenth weeks of crawling, from 2.17 to 2.73 in their thirteenth through last weeks of crawling, and from 2.38 to 2.71 in their first through thirteenth weeks of walking. Variety in locomotor methods was linked with the adaptiveness of infants' responses. Infants using more methods tended to have lower go ratios ($r = -.24$ for crawling and $-.43$ for walking).

Order of Emergence

In principle, from their first weeks of crawling, infants had the physical ability to refuse to attempt to go down risky downhill slopes that offered them the opportunity to utilize multiple descent methods. Avoidance was always available because it did not require new movements. In addition, parents' diaries and tests of milestones in the laboratory showed that all babies could move from their hands and knees to a prone sliding position, all could move from prone to sitting positions and vice versa, and all could execute the component movements of the backing method (moving into a prone position, pivoting 180°, and pushing backward). In fact, most infants performed these movements prior to crawling onset.

However, physical wherewithal did not translate directly to practice. The first appearance of each alternative "refusal" method in experimental-group

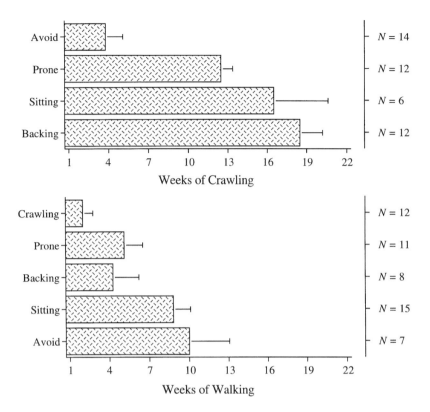

FIGURE 17.—Emergence of locomotor methods used on refusal trials on downhill slopes. Length of bars represents average number of weeks at first appearance over weeks of crawling and over weeks of walking. The number of infants (N) contributing data for each bar over crawling and walking appears to the right of each descent method. Error bars denote standard errors.

infants' repertoires was staggered over many weeks of crawling and walking. Figure 17 shows the average order of emergence for each descent method coded as refusals over weeks of crawling and walking. The number of experimental-group infants contributing data to group averages is shown on the right-hand side of the figure. (Note, in contrast, that Table 9 shows the total number of infants pooled across crawling and walking sessions.)

Avoidance was the first response that crawlers used to refuse to go down downhill slopes. In infants' first weeks of crawling, avoidance was the response coded on 100% of refusal trials. However, as new options entered their repertoires, children increasingly utilized various sliding positions, and the prevalence of the avoidance strategy therefore decreased steadily from 100% to 1% over weeks of crawling. Sliding prone appeared next as a refusal response, and the more "specialized" sitting and backing methods appeared latest, between experimental-group infants' sixteenth and nineteenth weeks of crawl-ing. Only six infants used the sitting method, but 12 used the backing method over weeks of crawling.

Before they began walking, most experimental-group infants had dem-onstrated multiple methods for coping with risky slopes. Their task, then, was to realize the utility of these methods for coping with risky slopes as walkers. On average, crawling appeared first as a form of refusal, followed by sliding prone and backing. Only 12 walkers responded by crawling, although every baby had crawled previously. Sitting and avoiding appeared last. Every infant eventually used the sitting method as walkers, but only seven resorted to avoidance. In fact, once infants had demonstrated the presence of an alterna-tive sliding position in their repertoires of methods for coping with slopes, avoidance became the least favored option, constituting less than 9% of re-fusal trials at each week of walking.

Exploring Locomotor Methods by Shifts in Position

A potential influence on infants' selection of one locomotor method over another was an additional type of exploratory activity on the starting platform. Similar to the means-ends exploration observed in object tasks (e.g., Piaget, 1952; Willatts, 1989), infants sometimes explored various loco-motor methods before going onto slopes by executing multiple shifts in posi-tion.

Uphill Shifts

Overall, multiple shifts during uphill trials were extremely rare. Figure 18a illustrates this point clearly because the average number of shifts never exceeded 0.50. (The horizontal lines at 1.0 in Figure 18 demarcate the differ-ence between single and multiple shifts.) On refusal trials, crawlers tended to switch from prone to a sitting position and wait out the remainder of the trial. Walkers tended to switch directly from upright to quadruped and climb up the hill. The number of shifts made by experimental-group infants ranged from none to six; multiple-shift trials tended to include repetitive shifts be-tween crawling and sitting positions.

Downhill Shifts

Multiple shifts were more frequent on descending trials and increased with weeks of crawling and walking. As shown in Figure 18b, the average num-ber of shifts exceeded 1.0 in experimental-group infants' sixteenth, nine-teenth, and last weeks of crawling and in their thirteenth week of walk-

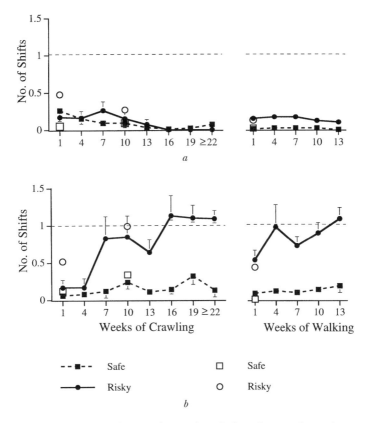

FIGURE 18.—Shifts in position on the starting platform by experimental-group (filled symbols) and control-group (open symbols) infants over weeks of crawling and walking. Trials grouped into safe (dashed lines) and risky (solid lines) hills relative to infants' slope boundaries. Infants tested multiple positions before starting onto hills at weeks when average number of shifts per trial was greater than 1.0 (indicated by horizontal, dashed lines). Error bars represent standard errors. *a,* Uphill. *b,* Downhill.

ing. Shifts made by experimental-group infants ranged from none to eight; multiple-shift trials tended to include different rather than repetitive positions.

In general, downhill shifts were associated with refusals and increased levels of visual and haptic exploration. Over weeks of crawling and walking, curves for shifts in position mirror go ratio curves (cf. Figure 11 above with Figure 18). Most multiple-shift (77%) and single-shift (99%) trials of experimental-group infants resulted in refusals, suggesting that infants shifted position *after* deciding that hills were risky for their typical locomotor methods. Infants shifted once if they had a readily available alternative, multiple times if they did not. In most cases (75%), multiple-shift trials resulted in the selection of an alternative sliding position rather than avoidance. The number of shifts was positively correlated with latency over weeks of crawling and walking (average $r = .52$). Likewise, shifts were positively correlated with touching over weeks of crawling and walking (average $r = .32$).

Experimental-group infants showed an additional type of means-ends behavior: using the posts at the corners of the starting platform near the top of the hill. Crawlers rarely touched the corner posts (1.1% of shift trials). However, walkers occasionally held onto the posts while shifting position (10.3% of shift trials), appearing to use the posts for support as an adult would grasp a railing on a tricky patch of ground. The only other occasion when infants attended to the posts was while touching slopes with their feet. Use of the posts is another form of means-ends behavior because, like simple tool use, it requires infants to see one structure or action as a means toward accomplishing a goal.

Summary: Locomotor Methods

Overall, infants evinced flexibility, choosing among various sliding positions to go down risky slopes. They spontaneously tested alternative options by shifting positions on the starting platform, and they consistently preferred an active climbing or sliding position to avoidance.

EFFECTS OF PRACTICE WITH SLOPES: EXPERIMENTAL- VERSUS CONTROL-GROUP INFANTS

The data yielded the quite surprising finding that changes in infants' ability to cope with slopes did not result from experience on slopes in the laboratory. Overall, comparisons between experimental- and control-group infants showed no differences despite experimental-group infants' exposure to hundreds of trials on slopes in repeated sessions over their first year and a half of life. Although changes in all infants' behavior were related to the duration of their everyday crawling and walking experience, there was no evidence that infants' responses depended on specific experience with slopes.

Slope Boundaries

Infants' physical ability to go up and down hills did not result from practice effects in the laboratory. As shown in Figure 9 above, experimental-group (filled symbols) and control-group (open symbols) infants had nearly identical uphill and downhill slope boundaries at each of the three matched sessions (the first and tenth weeks of crawling and the first week of walking).

84

Statistical comparisons revealed differences only for uphill boundaries in infants' first week of walking ($t[25] = 2.41$, $p < .05$). However, group means were very similar ($M = 8.53°$ and $11.50°$ for experimental- and control-group infants, respectively), and practice effects would have predicted the opposite outcome (higher boundaries for experimental-group infants).

Go Ratios

Adaptive responding did not result from experience with laboratory slopes. As shown in Figure 11 above, go ratios of experimental-group (filled symbols) and control-group (open symbols) infants were nearly identical on safe and risky uphill and downhill slopes. There were no statistical differences for any of the comparisons between groups at the three matched sessions (all p's > .10).

Age-Matched Comparisons

Comparisons between infants in the current longitudinal study and infants in previous cross-sectional studies provide additional evidence that changes in downhill go ratios did not depend on experience with laboratory slopes. At 8.5 months, infants in the current longitudinal study appeared comparable to the reckless 8.5-month-old crawlers described in previous research (Adolph et al., 1993a). In the cross-sectional sample, infants had one downhill trial each at 10°, 20°, 30°, and 40°. Eleven experimental-group infants in the current study could crawl at 8.5 months. The percentage of infants attempting to crawl down shallow and steep hills was similar in both groups. Every infant in the longitudinal study and 96% of infants in the cross-sectional study attempted 10° slopes; 45% of the former and 46% of the latter attempted the steepest slopes (36° and 40°, respectively).

Likewise, at 14 months, walking infants in the current longitudinal study looked very similar to the adaptive 14-month-old toddlers described in Adolph's (1995) cross-sectional sample. Both studies used the identical staircase procedure and go ratio index. Twelve experimental-group infants in the current study could walk at 14 months. Downhill walking boundaries were comparable across experiments ($M = 11.83°$ and $15.29°$ for infants in the longitudinal and the cross-sectional studies, respectively). Go ratios showed similar patterns for both groups. Average go ratios for infants in both studies were 0.49 on the $+5°$ group of slopes, slightly steeper than infants' slope boundaries. Go ratios decreased to 0.14 for infants in the longitudinal and to 0.11 for infants in the cross-sectional study on impossibly steep slopes in the $+18°$ range.

Exploratory Activity and Locomotor Methods

Infants' laissez-faire approach to ascent and more cautious behavior prior to descent were not the result of weekly experience with slopes in the laboratory. As shown in Figure 14 above, experimental-group (filled symbols) and control-group (open symbols) infants showed the same patterns of latency and touching at each of the three matched sessions. Both groups of infants hesitated and touched uphill slopes indiscriminately in their first weeks of crawling; both groups explored more on risky downhill slopes than safe ones over weeks of crawling, and both groups showed low levels of exploration in their first week of walking. Statistical comparisons suggested group differences only for touching safe downhill slopes in infants' first week of crawling, when both groups had comparable experience with slopes ($M =$ .44 and .28 for experimental- and control-group infants, respectively; $t[20] = 2.01$, $p < .058$). Likewise, experimental- and control-group infants showed similar patterns in frequency of shifts in position (see Figure 18). Statistical comparisons showed significant group differences only for safe downhill slopes at infants' first walking session ($M = .09$ and .01 for experimental- and control-group infants, respectively; $t[25] = 2.06$, $p < .05$). Variability in shifts was high at infants' first week of crawling, and there were no significant group differences (all p's > .10).

VII. DEVELOPMENTAL CORRELATES

The preceding chapter showed that infants' ability to cope with slopes was related to the duration of their locomotor experience. Overall, infants' slope boundaries, go ratios, exploratory activity, and flexibility of locomotor methods changed over weeks of crawling and walking. However, with each week of locomotor experience, infants got older, their bodies grew, their proficiency at moving on flat ground improved, and they had more experience with ascent and descent tasks at home.

The first section of this chapter describes changes in developmental *correlates of locomotor experience*. As above, change in each variable is plotted against weeks of crawling and walking experience. The second section describes intercorrelations between predictors and compares *effects of developmental factors* on infants' performance in the slope task. The third section examines *cross-situational transfer*.

Of special interest among the effects of developmental factors were independent effects of age and locomotor experience on downhill risky go ratios, the primary index of adaptive responding. Because the longitudinal design of the study controlled for duration of locomotor experience, and because infants contributed different numbers of crawling and walking sessions, statistical comparisons between predictors are presented for only two developmental checkpoints flanking the transition from crawling to walking: infants' *final* crawling session (the session prior to walking onset) and their *first* walking session. At infants' final crawling session, both crawling experience and age varied freely, allowing direct comparisons between the two variables. Locomotor experience ranged from 0.7 to 36.3 weeks, and age ranged from 9.8 to 14.6 months. In addition, there was a range in go ratios from 0 to 1.0. At infants' first walking session, walking experience was constant by definition, but test age ranged from 9.5 to 15.3 months, and go ratios ranged from 0.18 to 1.0. All experimental-group infants and one control-group baby contributed data to the final week of crawling, and both experimental- and control-group infants contributed data to the first week of walking (different sample size accounts for the discrepancy in minimum ages). Finally, parents' diaries and laboratory testing on stairs and slopes provided a unique opportunity to examine infants' behavior across multiple ascent/descent tasks.

CORRELATES OF LOCOMOTOR EXPERIENCE

Test Age and Onset Age

Owing to differences in infants' age at crawling and walking onset, there was a wide range in age within infants' first crawling (5.0 months) and walking (5.6 months) sessions. Younger ages at crawling onset and older ages at walking onset were associated with longer durations of crawling experience; age at crawling onset was negatively correlated with days of crawling experience ($r[25] = -.58$, $p < .001$), and age at walking onset was positively correlated with days of crawling experience ($r[25] = .57$, $p < .001$). The 15 experimental- and control-group infants who belly crawled prior to crawling on their hands and knees had more total crawling experience than the 14 babies who went directly to hands and knees crawling ($M = 5.5$ and 3.9 months, respectively; $t[25] = -2.90$, $p < .003$). In other words, longtime crawlers had a potential advantage for adaptive responding as walkers—they had more time to consolidate knowledge as crawlers, and they were older at their first walking session.

Crawling and Walking Proficiency on Flat Ground

Experimental- and control-group infants' locomotor proficiency on flat ground showed improvements over weeks of crawling and walking (see Figure 19). Crawlers' velocity increased, and their number of crawling cycles decreased, meaning that they executed faster movements and larger crawling steps (Vereijken et al., 1995). Likewise, walkers' step lengths increased, and their step widths decreased, indicating better postural control during periods of single-limb support (e.g., Bril & Breniere, 1992a, 1992b). Statistical comparisons confirmed improvements in measures of proficiency across progressive crawling and walking sessions (Table 10): very experienced crawlers were more skillful at locomotion prior to walking onset. There were no significant differences between experimental- and control-group infants at their first or tenth weeks of crawling or at their first week of walking. However, experimental-group infants tended to have more cycles than control-group infants at their first crawling session ($M = 6.86$ and 5.09, respectively; $t[20] = 1.99$, $p < .06$).

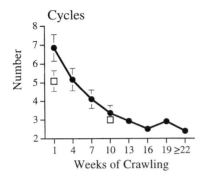
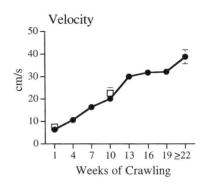

a

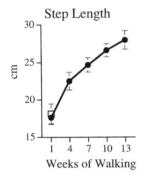
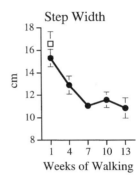

b

FIGURE 19.—Changes in locomotor proficiency on flat ground of experimental-group (filled symbols) and control-group (open symbols) infants over weeks of crawling and walking. Error bars denote standard errors. *a*, Crawling. *b*, Walking.

TABLE 10

VALUE OF *t* OBTAINED IN COMPARISONS OF LOCOMOTOR PROFICIENCY OVER
PROGRESSIVE TEST SESSIONS

| | | PAIRED *t* | | | | PAIRED *t* | |
| | | | | | | Step | Step |
	N	Cycles	Velocity		*N*	Length	Width
Weeks of crawling:				Weeks of walking:			
1st vs. 10th ...	10	5.42***	−8.43***	1st vs. 10th ...	12	−7.38***	4.12**
10th vs. 22d ...	8	1.46	−4.52**				

NOTE.—Sample includes only experimental-group infants contributing data to both comparison sessions. Sample size varies because of missed test sessions and different amounts of crawling experience.

** $p < .01$.

*** $p < .001$.

Body Dimensions

Several researchers have suggested that the dimensions of infants' bodies are related to their ability to crawl and to walk (e.g., Shirley, 1931; Thelen, 1984). As infants grow larger, their proportions become less top-heavy, and the ratio of muscle to fat increases (e.g., Behrman, 1992). Slimmer body proportions and increased strength coincide with improvements in locomotor skill and may facilitate the developmental shift from crawling on four limbs to walking upright (Shirley, 1931; Thelen, 1984). The principle reasons for this are that young infants' body fat outstrips their muscle strength and that their top-heavy proportions make it difficult to maintain balance. Similarly, differences in infants' body dimensions may make it more difficult to execute exploratory procedures and to crawl and walk over slopes. In this study, measures of weight and height provide an overall index of size. Leg length and head circumference provide more detailed indices of body proportions, and the Ponderal index relates height and weight in an overall chubbiness index.

There was a wide range in infants' initial sizes and in their rate of growth. Bigger, fatter babies tended to achieve each locomotor milestone later than smaller infants. Measures of height and leg length were positively correlated with age at crawling and walking onset (values of r ranged from .38 to .73, all p's < .05). In addition, measures of weight and head circumference were positively correlated with age at onset of crawling (values of r were .52 and .58, respectively, all p's < .02).

As expected, every experimental- and control-group infant got bigger and heavier across test sessions, and the Ponderal index decreased (see Figure 20). Statistical comparisons confirmed steady growth across sessions, meaning that longtime crawlers were more maturely proportioned prior to walking onset (see Table 11). There were no significant differences between experimental- and control-group infants at matched sessions. However, experimental-group infants tended to have larger heads (M = 48.11 centimeters) than controls (M = 46.73 centimeters) at infants' first week of walking ($t[25]$ = 2.82, p < .054). (Note that both Figure 20 and Table 11 support the general growth trend of larger, more cylindrical bodies. Discrepancies between the figure and the table in curves given for head circumference and the Ponderal index result from reduced sample size in the paired comparisons. In addition, as described below, experimental-group infant E-08 had an unusually large head. His data are responsible for the group differences between experimental- and control-group infants.)

Home Experience with Ascent and Descent

Although results indicated that infants' behavior on slopes did not depend on specific experience going up and down hills in the laboratory, in-

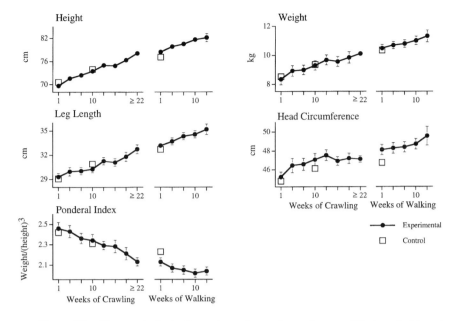

FIGURE 20.—Changes in body dimensions of experimental-group (filled symbols) and control-group (open symbols) infants over weeks of crawling and walking. Error bars denote standard errors.

TABLE 11

VALUE OF t OBTAINED IN COMPARISONS OF BODY DIMENSIONS OVER PROGRESSIVE TEST SESSIONS

	Paired t				
	Height	Weight	Head	Legs	Ponderal Index
Weeks of crawling:					
1st vs. 10th	−10.00***	−5.48***	−5.87***	−4.26**	1.62
	(10)	(10)	(9)	(10)	(10)
10th vs. ≥ 22d	−5.89***	−4.67**	−5.94***	−8.46***	3.76**
	(8)	(8)	(7)	(8)	(8)
Transition weeks:					
≥ 22d crawl vs. 1st walk ...	−.95	−1.12	−2.91*	−2.17	.20
	(8)	(8)	(8)	(8)	(8)
Weeks of walking:					
1st vs. 10th	−12.99***	−4.88***	−7.44***	−8.02***	6.17***
	(14)	(13)	(14)	(14)	(13)

NOTE.—Sample size, given in parentheses, includes only experimental-group infants contributing data to both comparison sessions. Sample size varies because of missed test sessions and different amounts of crawling experience.
* $p < .05$.
** $p < .01$.
*** $p < .001$.

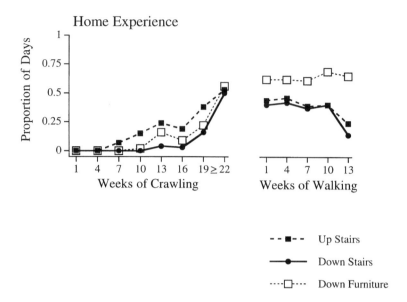

FIGURE 21.—Three measures of home experience with ascent and descent for experimental-group infants. Curves represent average proportion of days infants went on stairs or furniture between test sessions.

fants did have experience with ascent and descent in everyday situations at home. Parents' diaries reported days of experience going up and down household stairs and furniture and the methods that infants used to go up and to go down. Children with home experience went up stairs in a clambering position, down stairs in backing or sitting positions, and down furniture in a backing position. Frequency of exposure to ascent and descent was constrained by the layout of infants' homes and day-care centers and by parents' decisions to allow their infants access to various ascent and descent situations. For example, most parents of beginning crawlers "baby-proofed" their homes by gating household stairs, and most parents permitted children to go up stairs before they allowed them to come down. Coders scored frequency of experience with ascent and descent as the number of entries in parents' diaries between each crawling session and the number of entries between each walking session divided by the total number of days between sessions.

As shown in Figure 21, home experience with ascent and descent increased over weeks of crawling and over weeks of walking. At best, infants were exposed to home stairs and furniture on approximately half the days between test sessions, and longtime crawlers were at an advantage for home ascent/descent experience. In addition, infants tended to have more experience going up stairs than going down as crawlers and more experience descending furniture than descending stairs as walkers.

COMPARISONS BETWEEN DEVELOPMENTAL FACTORS AND
INFANTS' PERFORMANCE ON SLOPES

Final Crawling Session

As expected, many predictor variables were intercorrelated at infants' final crawling session (see Table 12). Locomotor experience and age were well correlated, and both variables show similar patterns of correlations with other predictors. More experienced, older crawlers were more proficient on flat ground and slopes, were taller and more evenly proportioned, and had more home experience with ascent and descent (read down the columns for experience and age in Table 12). More proficient crawlers were better on flat ground and on slopes, suggesting that estimates of slope boundaries were reliable (read down the columns for crawling proficiency). More proficient crawlers also tended to be taller, thinner, and more evenly proportioned, and they tended to have accumulated more home experience on stairs and furniture. Bigger babies were larger in all dimensions, but size did not predict home experience with ascent and descent (see the columns for body dimensions). Finally, home experience in each ascent/descent task was related to other home tasks (see the columns for home experience).

More important, crawling experience, test age, crawling proficiency on flat ground, and experience with home stairs were all correlated with go ratios on risky downhill slopes at infants' final crawling session (see Table 13). The strongest predictors of adaptive responding were measures of locomotor proficiency. Using stepwise multiple regression, both cycles and uphill slope boundaries were significant predictors of go ratios ($R^2[2, 11] = .75$). However, proficiency, experience, and age measures were intercorrelated. In order to compare the independent effects of age and experience, additional analyses were conducted in which either test age or locomotor experience was forced into the equation first. When crawling experience was forced into the equation first, multiple R was moderately strong ($R^2[1, 12] = .55$), and test age did not explain additional variance. In subsequent steps, only cycles accounted for additional unexplained variance ($R^2[2, 11] = .71$). When test age was forced into the equation first, multiple R was relatively low ($R^2[1, 12] = .39$), and crawling experience explained additional variance ($R^2[2, 11] = .60$). With both age and experience in the equation, no other variables explained additional variance. Thus, crawling experience was a stronger predictor of adaptive responding than infants' age.

First Walking Session

Intercorrelations between developmental factors at infants' first walking session showed similar patterns to those at infants' final crawling session (see

TABLE 12

FINAL CRAWLING SESSION: INTERCORRELATIONS BETWEEN CRAWLING EXPERIENCE, AGE, CRAWLING PROFICIENCY, BODY DIMENSIONS, AND HOME EXPERIENCE

	EXPER.	AGE	CRAWLING PROFICIENCY					BODY DIMENSIONS					HOME EXPERIENCE	
			Cycles	Veloc.	Up Bnd.	Down Bnd.	Height	Weight	Leg	Head	PI	Up Stairs	Down Stairs
Age	.65**												
Cycles	−.64**	−.82***											
Veloc.	.70**	.70**	−.79**										
Up bnd.	.79***	.49†	−.56*	.78***									
Down bnd.	.46†	.52*	−.42	.28	.53*								
Height	.54*	.69**	−.73**	.66**	.55**	.38							
Weight	.22	.29	−.53*	.29	.17	.04	.79***						
Leg	.34	.65**	−.73**	.37	.22	.30	.79***	.70***					
Head	−.06	.10	−.46†	.42	.16	.09	.51*	.68**	.36				
PI	−.56*	−.70**	−.48†	−.69**	−.66**	−.56*	−.58*	.04	−.35	.05			
Up stairs	.69**	.55*	−.42	.40	.39	.22	.25	.16	.33	−.02	−.23		
Down stairs ...	.55*	.47†	−.20	.27	.33	.22	.03	−.04	−.01	−.12	−.12	.79***	
Down furn.	.73**	.59*	−.47†	.46†	.40	.15	.33	.21	.46†	−.04	−.34	.84***	.64*

NOTE.—For correlations with crawling cycles, velocity, and home experience, $N = 15$; for all other correlations, $N = 16$. Exper. = experience. Veloc. = velocity. Up bnd. = uphill boundary. Down bnd. = downhill boundary. PI = Ponderal index. Down furn. = down furniture.

† $p < .10$.
* $p < .05$.
** $p < .01$.
*** $p < .001$.

TABLE 13

FINAL CRAWLING SESSION: CORRELATIONS BETWEEN DEVELOPMENTAL FACTORS AND
GO RATIOS ON RISKY DOWNHILL SLOPES

	CORRELATIONS WITH GO RATIOS ON RISKY DOWNHILL SLOPES			CORRELATIONS WITH GO RATIOS ON RISKY DOWNHILL SLOPES	
	r	N		r	N
Crawling experience	−.62*	16	Body dimensions:		
Test age	−.50*	16	Weight	−.26	16
Crawling proficiency:			Head	.09	16
Cycles	.77***	15	Legs	−.35	16
Velocity	−.62*	15	Ponderal index	.18	16
Uphill boundary	−.54*	16	Home experience:		
Downhill boundary ...	−.17	16	Up stairs	−.55*	15
Body dimensions:			Down stairs	−.45†	15
Height	−.36	16	Down furniture	−.43	15

† $p < .10$.
* $p < .05$.
*** $p < .001$.

Table 14). Note that walking experience was constant across infants by definition. Older walkers were taller (and thus had longer legs) and had more
home experience with ascent and descent (read down the column for age).
Bigger babies were larger in all dimensions, but size did not predict home
experience with ascent and descent (see the columns for body dimensions).
Amount of home experience in each ascent/descent task was related to experience with other home tasks (see the columns for home experience). However, in contrast with those of crawling, measures of walking proficiency on
flat ground were not intercorrelated and were not related to proficiency on
slopes, although the correlation between uphill and downhill boundaries was
significant, suggesting that boundary estimates were reliable. The low correlations between boundaries and other measures likely were due to the small
range in slope boundaries.

More critical, infants' test age and home experience with ascent and descent were correlated with risky go ratios at infants' first walking session (see
Table 15). Using stepwise multiple regression, home experience descending furniture and ascending stairs was a significant predictor of go ratios
($R^2[2, 10] = .75$), and test age did not explain additional variance. However,
test age was correlated with home experience. To assess the effect of experience independent of age, age was entered into the equation first. Multiple
R was relatively low ($R^2[1, 11] = .38$), and home experience descending furniture explained additional unique variance ($R^2[2, 10] = .59$). Thus, home
experience was the most important predictor of adaptive responding.

95

TABLE 14

First Walking Session: Intercorrelations Between Age, Walking Proficiency, Body Dimensions, and Home Experience

| | Age | Walking Proficiency | | | | Body Dimensions | | | | | Home Experience | |
		Stp. Len.	Stp. Wid.	Up Bnd.	Down Bnd.	Height	Weight	Leg	Head	PI	Up Stairs	Down Stairs
Stp. len.	.33											
Stp. wid.	−.31	−.07										
Up bnd.	.09	.03	−.24									
Down bnd.	.05	.15	−.26	.47*								
Height	.38*	.11	.07	−.18	−.24							
Weight	.32	−.13	−.16	−.10	−.26	.71***						
Leg	.51**	.15	−.20	−.15	−.15	.81***	.69***					
Head	.26	−.22	−.13	−.01	.03	.50**	.67***	.46*				
PI	.17	−.24	−.28	.18	.04	−.66***	.06	−.40*	−.02			
Up stairs	.60*	.66*	.11	−.17	.16	.27	.15	.43	.07	−.18		
Down stairs	.63*	.64*	.09	−.09	.19	.28	.14	.43	.08	−.22	.99***	
Down furn.	.70**	.71**	−.36	−.10	.20	.44†	.28	.46†	.10	−.23	.64**	.64**

Note.—For correlations with step length and step width, $N = 15$; for home experience, $N = 25$; for all other correlations, $N = 27$. Stp. len. = step length. Stp. wid. = step width. For other abbreviations, see Table 12.

† $p < .10$.
* $p < .05$.
** $p < .01$.
*** $p < .001$.

TABLE 15

First Walking Session: Correlations between Developmental Factors and
Go Ratios on Risky Downhill Slopes

	Correlations with Go Ratios on Risky Downhill Slopes			Correlations with Go Ratios on Risky Downhill Slopes	
	r	N		r	N
Test age.	−.46*	27	Body dimensions:		
Walking proficiency			Head	−.28	27
Step length	.09	25	Legs	.04	27
Step width	.03	25	Ponderal index	−.05	27
Uphill boundary	.19	27	Home experience:		
Downhill boundary . . .	−.03	27	Up stairs	−.61*	15
Body dimensions:			Down stairs	−.61*	15
Height	−.19	27	Down furniture	−.63*	15
Weight	−.30	27			

* $p < .05$.

CROSS-SITUATIONAL TRANSFER

The data on home experience provided a unique arena for examining transfer from one situation to another. The strongest evidence for cross-situational transfer would be tight coupling between infants' behavior at home and their performance on laboratory slopes. Two kinds of transfer were possible: (1) general, flexible knowledge for discriminating safe from risky surfaces for ascent and descent and (2) transfer of specialized locomotor methods from one descent task to another. The correlations between frequency of home experience and go ratios on slopes, especially at infants' first walking session, suggest the former, general transfer effect. That is, practice judging possibilities for locomotion over home stairs and furniture may have facilitated adaptive go ratios in the more novel situation with slopes.

Furthermore, the data suggest that transfer was limited to the more general type. Evidence for the latter scenario would be close timing in appearance of locomotor methods in multiple descent tasks (home stairs, lab stair, furniture, and slopes). For example, the simultaneous or closely linked appearance of the backing method in multiple descent tasks would suggest positive transfer for that particular locomotor method (in under 28 days, the maximum time between test sessions).

Results indicate that discovery of a new locomotor method in descent tasks at home did not transfer to descent tasks in the laboratory, and vice versa. In addition, there was no evidence that descent methods transferred from lab stair to lab slopes, although both tasks were tested at the same ses-

97

sion. Emergence of particular descent methods was widely spaced across tasks. Although most children eventually used backing in multiple situations, the average absolute difference between pairwise comparisons of infants' age at first use of backing was well over 28 days (M's ranged from 32.33 to 60.77 days) in all but the two most similar tasks, home stairs and lab stair ($M = 21.8$ days). Similarly, many children used the sitting position to descend slopes and the lab stair, but there was nearly 2 months' difference in its first appearance ($M = 64.67$ days). Only two children used sitting to descend home stairs, and they showed no evidence of transfer to descent of the lab stair or slopes (M's $= 59.0$ and 78.0 days, respectively).

SUMMARY: DEVELOPMENTAL FACTORS

How might interrelated developmental factors affect behavior in the slope task? The data suggest that infants' age affected their size and that their changing body dimensions constrained their ability to crawl and walk over flat ground and slopes. Locomotor proficiency, in turn, may affect the frequency and variety of infants' home experience with locomotion, providing a generalized context for learning to control balance on different supporting surfaces. In addition, parents may take infants' age, changing locomotor proficiency, and more grown-up-looking bodies into account when structuring the home environment and exposure to various descent tasks. Moreover, infants' experience—duration of crawling experience and exposure to ascent/descent tasks at home—was a stronger predictor of risky go ratios than test age. The results of both Chapter VI and Chapter VII point to the important role that locomotor experience plays in adaptive responding in a novel locomotor task. The next chapter lends further support to these findings by examining individual differences in responding.

VIII. INDIVIDUAL DIFFERENCES

Individual differences are an important part of understanding change because they highlight the range in normal development and the different paths that development can take. Individual differences in onset age and locomotor proficiency are widely documented in the literature. Some infants crawl or walk sooner than others (e.g., Frankenburg & Dodds, 1967; McGraw, 1935; Shirley, 1931), and, matched for age or locomotor experience, some infants crawl or walk better than others (e.g., Bril & Breniere, 1989). Likewise, in the current study, there was a wide range in infants' age at the onset of locomotor milestones and in their locomotor proficiency.

Few studies, however, have described individual differences in adaptive locomotor responses. For example, earlier cross-sectional research with 14-month-old walkers showed strong individual differences in the adaptiveness of infants' responses to slopes, especially on downhill trials (Adolph, 1995). In that study, individual differences were assessed according to the slope where go ratios decreased below 0.50 and remained consistently low. Most toddlers (55%) were extremely cautious, with a sharp decrease in go ratios below 0.50 at +5° and all steeper slopes; 6% were more liberal, with a decrease in go ratios at +13°; 26% were quite bold, with high go ratios until the steepest +18° slopes; and 13% were uniformly reckless, responding indiscriminately, with high go ratios above 0.50 at every slope increment. Exploratory activity precisely mirrored go ratios on risky downhill slopes, pointing to corresponding differences in infants' ability to obtain relevant information from exploratory activity. On hills where hesitation, touching, and shifting increased, go ratios decreased. The current study expands on these findings with a comprehensive portrayal of stable individual differences over many months of testing.

UPHILL GO RATIOS

All infants were uniformly reckless at uphill sessions throughout the duration of the study. Go ratios were consistently high (above 0.50 with the

99

two-group safe/risky method), and exploratory activity was consistently low. Individual differences were restricted to differences in children's slope boundaries, rather than patterns of adaptive responding.

Given the change in downhill go ratios over weeks of crawling and walking, the uniform lack of caution displayed during ascent suggests that adaptive responding resulted from the different task constraints of going up and down, rather than from stable temperamental differences across tasks. In other words, there were no timid or fussy babies who were reticent about going over *both* uphill and downhill slopes.

DOWNHILL GO RATIOS

Although sample means showed two smooth go ratio curves for descent, examination of individual protocols revealed clear individual differences in patterns of responding. To examine individual differences in descent, experimental-group infants were grouped according to patterns of change in their go ratios across test sessions. Of central interest was transfer over the transition from crawling to walking. A criterion of 0.50 was used to assess adaptive responding and transfer, and the seven-slope-group technique was used for calculating go ratios. Go ratios less than or equal to 0.50 at all risky slopes ($+5°$, $+13°$, and $+18°$) reflected adaptive responding, go ratios less than or equal to 0.50 over the transition from crawling to walking at all risky slopes reflected transfer, and go ratios increasing from less than or equal to 0.50 to greater than 0.50 over the transition from crawling to walking reflected failure to transfer.

All experimental-group infants displayed one of three patterns: (1) adaptive responding as expert crawlers, no transfer from crawling to walking, and adaptive responding as experienced walkers (i.e., the pattern displayed by group averages and denoted as *no-transfer* infants below); (2) adaptive responding as crawlers, transfer from crawling to walking, and subsequent adaptive responding as walkers (denoted by *transfer* infants below); and (3) indiscriminate responding as crawlers and walkers (denoted by *indiscriminate* infants below). The following sections describe these three response patterns and examine factors that contributed to individual differences.

Like the group averages in Figure 11*b* above, 10 no-transfer infants (six boys and four girls) exhibited two go ratio curves on risky slopes, one after they began crawling, the other after they began walking. Figure 22*a* shows the no-transfer pattern on risky slopes with exemplar data from four of the no-transfer infants. Solid lines and filled circles represent $+5°$ slopes, dashed lines and open squares denote $+13°$ slopes, and dotted lines and open triangles denote $+18°$ slopes. Given the criteria for adaptive responding and transfer, the most important curve is the one at $+5°$. Infants E-04 and E-16 belly

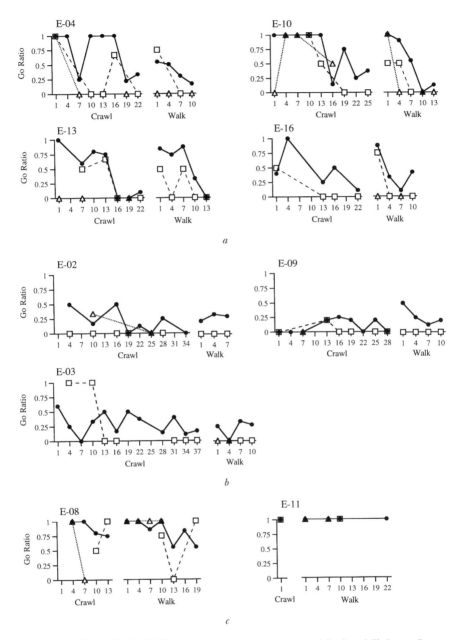

Figure 22.—Individual differences in response patterns on risky downhill slopes. Curves represent go ratios at +5° (filled circles and solid lines), +13° (open squares and dashed lines), and +18° (open triangles and dotted lines). *a*, Four representative infants from the no-transfer group. *b*, Three infants in the transfer group. *c*, Two infants in the indiscriminate group.

crawled prior to moving on their hands and knees, and E-10 and E-13 crawled only on their hands and knees. All no-transfer children had high go ratios in their first weeks of crawling and low go ratios by their last weeks of crawling. Note that E-16 had no data on risky hills at weeks 7 and 10 of crawling because his slope boundary was 36°.) Most important, every no-transfer infant showed a dramatic increase in go ratios over the transition from crawling to walking and a decrease in subsequent weeks of walking.

Three transfer infants (one boy and two girls) showed adaptive responding over weeks of crawling and walking, with no dramatic increase over the transition from crawling to walking (see Figure 22b). Infants E-02 and E-09 had consistently low go ratios (≤ 0.50) at each week of crawling, although both infants' errors decreased over weeks of crawling. E-03 showed the typical decrease from high go ratios to low ones from the first to the last weeks of crawling. Her data provide evidence that the transfer effect was not limited to infants always cautious about going down slopes. Go ratios for all three transfer infants remained low (≤ 0.50) over the transition from crawling to walking, although E-09 exhibited a short increase in errors at his first week of walking (0.50 at $+5°$), which quickly decreased in subsequent weeks.

The last two indiscriminate infants (one boy and one girl) showed no evidence of adaptive responding at all, either over weeks of crawling or over weeks of walking (see Figure 22c). Their data are especially interesting because maladaptive responding occurred for different reasons. E-11 treated downhill slopes the same as uphill, with a false alarm rate of 100% at every session, even in her twenty-third week of walking. She contributed few data points because she crawled for only 1 week and was out of town for several weeks of walking. E-08 responded haphazardly. Go ratios at $+5°$ never decreased below 0.50, and he sometimes refused risky hills closer to his slope boundary, then attempted hills more remote.

OTHER RESPONSE MEASURES

Measures of exploratory activity prior to descent suggested that individual differences in go ratios may have been due, in part, to differences in infants' propensity to obtain information relevant to coping with slopes. In general, all three individual difference groups displayed the same patterns of latency and touching exhibited by the sample as a whole: higher rates of prolonged exploration in the first weeks of crawling, a decrease over weeks of crawling, and lower levels of exploration over weeks of walking. However, over weeks of crawling, transfer infants tended to hesitate and touch more than no-transfer infants, and indiscriminate infants tended to hesitate and touch less than no-transfer infants. Both no-transfer and transfer infants showed a large increase in number of exploratory shifts in position. However,

TABLE 16

INDIVIDUAL DIFFERENCES IN DURATION OF CRAWLING EXPERIENCE
AND AGE AT WALKING

	Belly Crawled	Crawl Experience (Days)	Age at Walk (Days)
No transfer:			
E-01	✓	141	309
E-04	✓	172	350
E-05	✓	139	388
E-06	✓	207	367
E-10		186	399
E-12		148	408
E-13		162	345
E-14	✓	144	421
E-15		96	379
E-16	✓	161	453
Mean		155.60	381.90
Transfer:			
E-02	✓	242	421
E-03	✓	261	434
E-09	✓	200	422
Mean		234.33	425.67
Indiscriminate:			
E-08		94	342
E-11		12	304
Mean		53.00	323.00

transfer infants executed multiple shifts in positions at more weeks of crawling and walking (mean number of shifts > 1.0) than no-transfer infants. The two indiscriminate babies never executed multiple shifts.

Age and Locomotor Experience

Duration of crawling experience and age at walking onset revealed very different profiles for the three individual difference groups (see Table 16). There was no overlap in duration of crawling experience and age at walking onset between transfer and indiscriminate infants. Transfer babies were at an advantage in both cases, with the most crawling experience and the oldest age at walking onset. Indiscriminate infants were at a disadvantage, with the least crawling experience and the youngest age at walking onset. In addition, all three transfer infants had a prolonged period of belly crawling, and neither of the indiscriminate infants belly crawled. Infants in the no-transfer group lay squarely in the middle, with moderate amounts of crawling experience and respectable ages at walking onset; approximately half the no-transfer infants belly crawled, and half went straight to hands and knees crawling.

These group differences suggest that transfer infants benefited from their extra weeks of crawling and older age at walking and, conversely, that indiscriminate infants suffered from their minimal exposure to crawling and younger age at walking. In fact, effects of experience and age at infants' final crawling session revealed by regression analyses were due largely to the high go ratios of the two inexperienced, young indiscriminate infants. Likewise, regression effects for age at infants' first walking session were due largely to the low go ratios of the three older transfer infants. Additional evidence is provided by control-group infant C-07, who never crawled and walked early. Her go ratios were 1.0 at every safe and risky slope increment in her first and tenth weeks of walking.

Locomotor Proficiency

Infants' type of crawl (belly or hands and knees) and duration of crawling experience led to group differences in proficiency crawling down slopes and over flat ground. Belly crawling benefited the transfer and no-transfer infants on downhill slopes, where they had steeper boundaries than infants in the indiscriminate group, who crawled only on their hands and knees. In contrast, belly crawling hampered the transfer infants on flat ground, where they had more cycles than infants in the other two groups. No-transfer and transfer infants progressed to faster velocities and fewer cycles than indiscriminate infants, who crawled for only a short time.

Slope boundaries were similar over weeks of walking. All three individual difference groups showed the characteristic decrease in slope boundaries over the transition from crawling to walking and increase over weeks of walking. In their first few weeks of walking, transfer infants tended to be more proficient walkers on flat ground than infants in the other groups (the former manifesting longer step lengths and narrower step widths). Transfer infants' longer steps suggest better balance control from the start.

Body Dimensions

Differences in infants' age at crawling and walking onset were related to group differences in infants' body dimensions. At crawling onset, transfer infants tended to be younger and smaller than infants in the other two groups. At walking onset, transfer infants tended to be older and more maturely proportioned than infants in the other two groups.

A most striking individual difference was the size of indiscriminate infant E-08's head (51.9 centimeters at his fourth week of crawling). Despite his otherwise normal body build, E-08 had a very large head—the largest at each crawling and walking session. E-08 is the infant who sometimes refused and explored +5° slopes while speeding immediately down hills in even riskier ranges. A possible explanation for E-08's inconsistent behavior is that his large head threw him off balance when he attempted to explore steep hills or to go down them. E-08 sometimes did manage to crawl and walk down very steep hills, but he could not do it consistently enough to bring his slope boundaries up to par. In addition, E-08 exhibited the most dramatic falls of the sample, a sort of headfirst dive and rolling somersault as though he had pitched too far forward.

Home Experience

The most notable difference in home experience between groups was for the two indiscriminate infants. Neither infant had any home experience on stairs for the entire duration of the study, and they were the only experimental-group infants with no home stair experience. E-08's family did not have stairs inside their home, and his parents did not allow him to go up or down stairs in other situations. E-11's family did have household stairs, and the mother reported that the child was desperate to go up and down. However, E-11's parents considered her to be very reckless, and they did not allow her to go on stairs or to descend furniture. All three transfer infants had frequent experience going up and down stairs and furniture from their last weeks of crawling and in their first weeks of walking.

SUMMARY: INDIVIDUAL DIFFERENCES

Each experimental-group infant showed one of three patterns of responding. Like the group average, most infants had two go ratio curves over weeks of crawling and walking. However, three infants did show evidence of transfer over the transition from crawling to walking, and two babies responded indiscriminately across sessions. Transfer infants were, in general, more cautious about descending slopes than infants in the other groups, as evinced by lower go ratios and higher levels of exploration. However, transfer infants' consistently "smart" go ratios did not result from fussiness, laziness, or timidness. Two of the transfer infants had downhill crawling boundaries of 36°, and all of them actively explored slopes by looking, touching, and shifting positions. Transfer infants were no more likely to avoid risky hills than infants in the other groups.

The individual difference groups lend support to analyses of developmental factors. Although there were only a few infants in the transfer and indiscriminate groups, these children were at the extremes of the sample for duration of crawling experience, age at walking onset, crawling proficiency, body growth, and home experience. Transfer infants crawled longest and were most proficient by their final weeks; they were the oldest and most maturely proportioned at walking onset. Indiscriminate infants, in contrast, crawled for the shortest durations and were least proficient by their final weeks; they were youngest and most top-heavy at walking onset; in addition, they were the only infants with no experience on home stairs. In fact, the differences between transfer and indiscriminate infants were largely responsible for the effects of regression analyses at infants' final crawling session and first walking session.

IX. UNDERSTANDING CHANGE

The present research provides a detailed portrayal of the many faces of change in infant locomotion. The central framework for understanding these changes is a focus on adaptive locomotion—how infants match locomotor responses to the properties of the terrain relative to their own bodies and skills. Infants provide an especially apt illustration of adaptive locomotion because their bodies and locomotor skills change dramatically and many locomotor tasks are novel. The longitudinal design and staircase procedure of the current study captured these essential elements of change. In the slopes task, the only way for infants to make on-line decisions about whether ground was safe or risky was to obtain information from exploratory movements at the start of each trial. Exploration, in turn, was only part of the story. Infants also had to decide which method of locomotion to use. In this final chapter, I integrate the key findings of the current study with results from previous research and present a developmental theory for understanding how infants acquire the ability to navigate the everyday environment.

THE PATH OF CHANGE IN ADAPTIVE RESPONDING

Results from this research point up the importance of frequent, longitudinal observations for studying change. By filling in the gaps left by previous cross-sectional experiments (Adolph, 1995; Adolph et al., 1993a), this study replicates and extends earlier findings. Young crawlers plunged headlong up and down safe and risky slopes alike, but older walkers knew when to walk and when to select an alternative locomotor method. Most important, between these end points was a discrete U-shaped function flanked by two continuous go ratio curves on risky slopes. Over weeks of crawling, infants distinguished safe downhill slopes from risky ones, and they discovered appropriate ways to achieve the landing platform. However, infants' knowledge did not transfer over the transition from crawling to walking. Rather, infants had to acquire all over again, at the same laborious pace, the ability to discriminate safe from risky hills as walkers.

Detailed analyses of go ratios, the primary index of adaptive responding, suggest a three-step progression for each method of locomotion. When infants first began crawling, their responses were most reckless, but they were not indiscriminate; go ratios on risky downhill slopes were high, but not quite as high as go ratios on safe downhill slopes or uphill slopes. After several weeks of crawling, infants' responses were most adaptive, with go ratios matched closely to the probability of success; downhill go ratios were low, and downhill slope boundaries were steep. Finally, longtime crawlers were overly cautious; go ratios remained low, but infants refused to crawl down perfectly safe hills that they had crawled down in previous sessions. Similarly, over weeks of walking, infants progressed from high but discriminating go ratios, to adaptive responding, to overly cautious judgments. Several walkers in previous cross-sectional samples also showed overly cautious judgments with go ratios in perfect step functions from shallow to steep hills (Adolph, 1995).

The puzzle is why beginning crawlers and walkers erred recklessly if they had some inkling that the steepest hills were risky and why experienced infants erred cautiously if they already had the ability to make finely tuned judgments. One explanation is a change from more liberal to more conservative response criteria. In fact, changing response criteria make good developmental sense. Beginning crawlers and walkers may be biased toward more liberal responding. Learning by doing is the fastest way to test the limits of a new skill, and infants would make little progress in the development of crawling and walking if they cautiously tested each step. Evolution and culture have provided caregivers who protect infants from the dire consequences of rash responding. Outside the laboratory, parents do not urge their newly mobile babies to negotiate risky terrain on their own. Over weeks of locomotor experience, infants' response criteria may become more realistic.

As infants discern more clearly the limits of their locomotor proficiency, they begin to match locomotor responses to the probability of success. During this period, parents in this study commented that infants made "smart" locomotor decisions regarding home stairs and furniture. Finally, after achieving some expertise with a new skill, infants may become biased toward more conservative, adult-like responding. Although athletes and daredevils push their limits in risky situations, typical pedestrians hedge their bets and err on the side of caution. We choose the bunny slope rather than the Olympic one. We slide carefully down a steep mountain path gripping branches for support rather than running down it at full speed. Once infants begin exhibiting adaptive responses, caregivers may provide them more freedom to solve locomotor problems on their own. For example, many parents removed the gates on household stairs and allowed infants daily access. Thus, the real, practical penalties for errors become more serious, and infants may notice parents' changing expectations and the changing consequences of high-risk errors.

Task Constraints

Infants' response criteria show increasing sensitivity to task constraints. Over weeks of crawling and walking, the difference between uphill and downhill slopes became more apparent. Infants were consistently reckless about going uphill, where the consequences of falling are minimal, and they became increasingly cautious about going downhill, where losing balance is more serious. Likewise, infants showed adaptive responses earlier in tasks such as the visual cliff, where the apparent penalty for error was high (e.g., Campos et al., 1978), than in tasks such as navigating through apertures or detouring around obstacles, where errors were not aversive (e.g., Palmer, 1987).

ARE CHANGES LEARNING?

Previous research linked adaptive responding in locomotor tasks with infants' age, locomotor status (whether they were crawlers or walkers), and locomotor experience. Older, more experienced infants avoided a visual cliff, detoured around obstacles, coped with visual and mechanical perturbations of balance in moving rooms or on moving floors, and exhibited more means-ends testing on stairs (e.g., Campos et al., 1992; Lockman, 1984; Shumway-Cook & Woollacott, 1985; Stoffregen et al., 1987; Ulrich et al., 1990). In addition, older walking infants behaved more adaptively than younger crawling infants on waterbeds and slopes (e.g., Adolph et al., 1993a; Gibson et al., 1987).

The current experiment was designed to pull apart these factors by observing infants longitudinally over the entire period of change. Overall, the preponderance of evidence indicates that locomotor experience was the primary correlate of change. If test age were responsible for adaptive responding, we would have observed one smooth decrease in errors over crawling and walking, rather than a discontinuous curve with an increase in errors at the transition between crawling and walking. If change in locomotor status from crawling to walking spurred adaptive responding, we would have observed a high error rate across weeks of crawling and an abrupt decrease in errors after walking onset. Further, direct comparisons between age and experience at infants' final crawling session showed stronger effects for experience. Likewise, comparisons between age and home experience at infants' first walking session showed stronger effects for home experience. These experience-related changes point to learning. However, although experience has a primary role in adaptive responding, age and locomotor status also play a part in facilitating change, as described below.

SPECIFICITY OF LEARNING

Experience-related learning was both impressively general and surprisingly specific. The evidence suggests that infants learned to judge slopes relative to their current level of crawling or walking proficiency. They responded differently to the same absolute degree of slant depending on fluctuating improvements and decrements in their crawling or walking abilities. However, learning was specific to the postural constraints and vantage point of infants' typical method of locomotion.

The general nature of learning is shown by the steady decrease in go ratios over changes *within* infants' typical method of locomotion—changes in crawling proficiency, changes in walking proficiency, and changes from belly crawling to moving on their hands and knees (see Figures 9 and 11 above). In particular, slope boundaries marked a division between safe and risky hills in such a way that an impossibly steep hill at one week of crawling might be safe at the next week of crawling and a safe slope for belly crawling might be risky for crawling on hands and knees. A corresponding decrease in go ratios despite such changes in locomotor proficiency suggests that infants learned to make decisions by updating information about their current level of locomotor skill relative to the degree of slant.

Specificity of learning was evinced by failure to transfer *across* changes in infants' locomotor status (see Figure 11 above). The parallel shape of the two go ratio curves flanking the transition from crawling to walking suggests that learning was no faster the second time around (see Table 5 above). Moreover, infants showed failure to transfer over changes in vantage point, even from trial to trial. When new walkers faced hills from their old, familiar crawling position, they responded adaptively and slid down. But, when beginning walkers faced hills in their new upright position, many infants walked over the edge and fell (see Figure 13 above).

CHARACTERIZATION OF THE LEARNING PROCESS

Construction

A theory of experience-driven learning requires a characterization of the learning process. The most prevalent account of infant learning is an additive, enrichment process where knowledge is constructed via transformation of schema or simple associative pairing (e.g., Piaget, 1952; Rovee-Collier, Greco-Vigorito, & Hayne, 1993). A construction process implies that children build knowledge from the ground up by sequencing or reorganizing components in their repertoires. In object tasks, for example, work by Piaget (1952) and others suggests that infants may construct new, more adaptive actions when current behaviors or schemes do not satisfy the demands of the current situation. Accordingly, infants learned to operate a lever on a rotating turntable by progressively stringing together component movements into the appropriate sequence (Koslowski & Bruner, 1972).

In such locomotion tasks as obstacles, cliffs, and stairs, infants' means-ends exploration is consistent with an additive, construction process. Such means-ends behaviors as detours and experimentation with component movements appear slowly, become increasingly elaborated, and typically accompany new, more adaptive solutions (e.g., Campos et al., 1978; Lockman, 1984; Ulrich et al., 1990). In the slopes studies, means-ends exploration was indexed by infants' shifts in position on the starting platform. Consistent with a construction process, shifts appeared late in development, increased in amount and complexity, and were linked with adaptive responding (see Figure 18 above). In addition, exploratory shifts are consistent with the notion that infants may construct new descent methods—such as the backing position—from component movements already in their repertoires (e.g., moving from sitting to prone positions, pivoting 180°, and pushing backward). For example, in his seventh and thirteenth weeks of crawling, transfer infant E-09 tested multiple pivoting and backing positions on the starting platform. In subsequent weeks, he executed the backing position on the starting platform and slid down.

Differentiation

An alternative account of learning is that of a subtractive, sculpting process of gradual differentiation and selection (Gibson, 1969, 1988, 1991; Gibson & Gibson, 1955). A differentiation/selection process implies two things. First, in principle, the infant must be able to obtain essential information from the start of independent mobility and at the start of every trial. That is, physiological sensitivity and ability to execute appropriate exploratory movements are prerequisites for learning and on-line decision making. Second, a differentiation/selection process must show increasing specificity as behavior gradually narrows in to the essential information and the most functionally adaptive responses. Exploratory movements and locomotor responses should become more refined and efficient and less groping and floundering. In other words, given the raw materials, infants' job is to obtain the necessary information, understand its relevance for locomotion, and select an appropriate locomotor response. As described below, the evidence points to a long differentiation/selection process over months of locomotor development and a short differentiation/selection process in the time span of each trial.

Each task in the literature on infant locomotion indicates that infants do, in fact, possess the raw materials for differentiation learning. Long before infants become mobile, they show the physiological rudiments necessary for discriminating visual and mechanical information for surface properties and for controlling balance, as evinced by very simple forms of visual, oral, and manual responses. Prelocomotor infants show sensitivity to disparity in depth on a visual cliff (e.g., Bertenthal & Campos, 1987), differences between obstacles and apertures (e.g., Carrol & Gibson, 1981), simulated optic flow in a moving room (e.g., Butterworth & Hicks, 1977), mechanical perturbations of balance (e.g., Woollacott et al., 1987), visual and haptic information specifying rigidity (e.g., Gibson & Walker, 1984), and differences in surface slant (e.g., Slater & Morison, 1985).

Moreover, infants possess the ability to execute appropriate, more sophisticated exploratory movements at the start of mobility, meaning that the requisite information for guiding locomotion can, in fact, be obtained. The longitudinal data from the current study showed that infants began executing the full repertoire of exploratory looking and touching movements in their first weeks of crawling. Similarly, cross-sectional studies indicate that newly mobile infants can differentiate between surfaces on the basis of information obtained from exploratory looking and touching. Young crawlers, for example, exhibited more differential visual and haptic exploration on steep hills than on shallow ones in both locomotor and nonlocomotor tasks (Adolph et al., 1993a; Eppler et al., 1996). Likewise, young crawlers looked at and touched a pliant waterbed more than a rigid plywood surface (Gibson et al., 1987).

Consistent with a differentiation process, adaptive responses to safe and risky ground lag far behind exploratory looking and touching. In particular, learning the relevance that certain information holds for balance control may be a key hurdle for adaptive responding (Eppler et al., 1996). For example, in the current study, and in previous cross-sectional research, the same crawlers who explored steep and shallow hills differentially by looking and touching crawled over the edge of impossibly steep hills without testing a single alternative sliding position (Adolph et al., 1993a). Likewise, the same crawlers who explored waterbeds and rigid surfaces differentially crossed both surfaces in equal numbers (Gibson et al., 1987). Despite their differential heart rates, beginning crawlers crossed the deep side of a visual cliff (Campos et al., 1992).

The selection of optimal alternatives may await the development of variety of strategic options in infants' repertoires. Apparently, young infants prefer to attempt any available method of locomotion rather than avoid going.

In the slopes task, avoidance virtually disappeared as new sliding positions entered infants' repertoires. Moreover, beginning crawlers may have little motivation to optimize outcomes in tasks where errors are not aversive. For example, beginning crawlers frequently chose impossibly narrow apertures (Palmer, 1987) or crawled straight toward an obstacle in the path (Lockman, 1984), but their errors resulted only in longer, less efficient paths. Crawlers attempted to traverse pliant waterbeds (Gibson et al., 1987) or to climb up impossibly high stairs (Ulrich et al., 1990), where the consequences of losing their balance were minimal. In fact, inefficiency and labor-intensive movements are characteristic of early periods of crawling and walking (McGraw, 1945). Presumably, if infants limited themselves to optimal movements rather than functionally workable ones, they would not display the range of arduous belly crawling, cruising, and walking patterns that are so typical of beginning crawlers and walkers, and expert crawlers would have no reason to become novice, poorly proficient walkers. Infants' first goal may be to move from one place to another; honing and perfecting movements may come later.

Summary of the Evidence

Figure 23 summarizes evidence from the current study for a differentiation/selection process in the development of on-line decision making. Figure 23*a–c* shows changes on downhill slopes over weeks of crawling and walking. Each graph is a thumbnail sketch of data presented in earlier chapters. Figure 23*a* shows go ratios, the overall index of adaptive responding. Figure 23*b* represents changes in exploratory activity, the informational basis of infants' responses. Figure 23*c* shows change in the functional outcome of exploratory movements. Finally, Figure 23*d* illustrates the process of differentiation and selection in the course of a single trial. This on-line decision-making process is discussed in detail in the final section of the *Monograph*.

As summarized in Figure 23*a*, change in infants' go ratios showed the strongest evidence of a differentiation/selection process. With each week of crawling and walking, go ratios narrowed in to infants' slope boundaries. Moreover, within sessions, infants' judgments were always most accurate on the riskiest hills most remote from their slope boundaries (see Figure 12 above); go ratios were always lowest at $+18°$ and highest at $+5°$. The most dramatic improvement across sessions was on hills slightly steeper than slope boundaries ($+5°$). Cross-sectional samples showed similar results (Adolph, 1995). Errors were highest on hills slightly steeper than infants' slope boundaries, and judgments were most accurate on the very steepest hills most remote from infants' slope boundaries.

Likewise, exploratory looking and touching showed a gradual differentia-

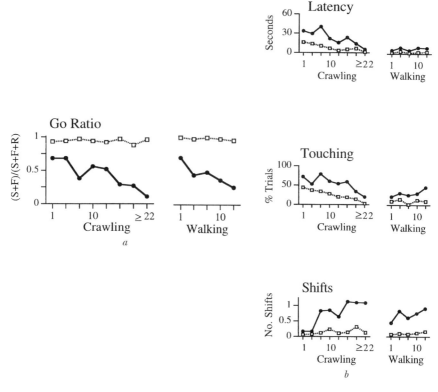

FIGURE 23.—Summary of developmental changes over weeks of crawling and walking and schematic description of on-line decision-making process. *a,* Overall index of adaptive responding and learning. Graph shows average go ratios on safe (dashed lines) and risky (solid lines) downhill slopes over weeks of crawling and walking. *b,* Informational basis of infants' decisions. Graphs show change in amount of exploratory activity on safe (dashed lines) and risky (solid lines) downhill trials over weeks of crawling and walking. *c,* Functional outcome of exploratory movements. The top three graphs show average go ratios on risky, downhill slopes after quick glances, long looks, and coordinated looking and touching. The bottom graph shows average percentage avoidance on trials when infants refused their typical method of locomotion. *d,* Schematic account of the on-line decision-making process in adaptive locomotion. Schematic represents infants' decision-making process in the course of a trial.

tion process. On slopes, levels of latency and touching were highest in infants' first weeks of crawling, and prolonged exploration was distributed across both safe and risky hills and uphill slopes as well as downhill ones (see Figure 23*b*). With weeks of crawling experience, prolonged looking and touching gradually geared in to downhill, risky slopes steeper than infants' slope boundaries. Moreover, the functional outcome of exploratory activity showed steady improvement (see Figure 23*c*). Over weeks of crawling and walking,

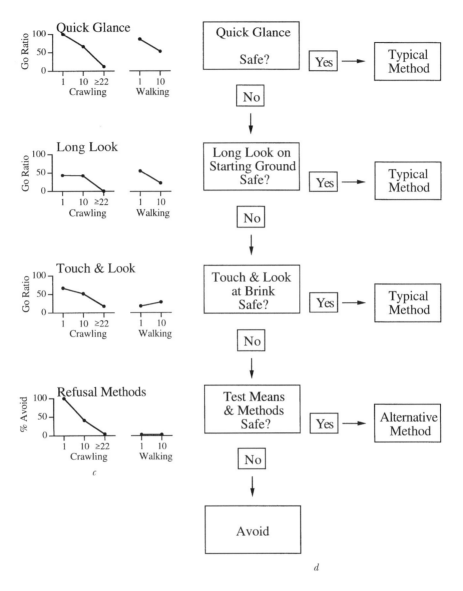

FIGURE 23 (*Continued*)

failures decreased following quick glances, long looks, and touches. The simultaneous refinement of exploratory looking and touching and decrease in errors suggests improvements in the efficiency of exploration and in relating the information obtained from exploratory movements to consequences for balance control. Apparently, infants distributed their exploratory movements

115

more selectively and benefited more from each type of movement. Likewise, in object tasks, adults showed similar patterns of decreasing amounts of exploration coupled with increasing improvements in judgments (Klatzky et al., 1989). As visual and haptic exploration improved, infants showed more flexible use of alternative descent methods. Shifts in position were followed by refusals, and avoidance responses were replaced by more functionally effective sliding positions.

ORIGIN OF NEW MOVEMENTS AND THE IMPETUS FOR CHANGE

Various exploratory movements and descent methods were part of the knowledge base that infants brought to the slope task. Thus, a central problem for a differentiation/selection theory of learning is an account of how so much knowledge becomes available so early. Presumably, if prolonged exploration in infants' first weeks of crawling resulted from deliberate forethought, beginning crawlers should also have shown adaptive responses on perilously risky hills. That is, if infants explored steep hills because they knew hills were risky, they should not have attempted to crawl down. It is unlikely that infants would search for new methods of locomotion on the off chance that these new movements would prove useful in a novel task. How, then, might infants acquire the tools for learning and a repertoire of locomotor responses without knowing the payoff ahead of time? What is the origin of infants' exploratory movements and descent methods, and what factors instigate their discovery?

Data from the current study argue against two commonsense explanations for learning. As described below, infants do not require explicit instruction to learn new ways of moving, nor do they require aversive consequences to spur the learning process. Rather, learning new ways to explore and traverse a ground surface may be overdetermined by the vicissitudes of development. More specifically, changes in locomotor proficiency, driven, in turn, by changes in infants' body dimensions, may give rise to different sorts of variability. With sufficient variability in the system, a differentiation/selection process can operate. In addition, with more exploratory movements and locomotor methods in their repertoires, infants have more ways to cope with task demands.

Explicit Instruction and Retrieval

A straightforward explanation for the origin of new movements is explicit instruction and retrieval. Infants might learn new movements from their parents and be prompted to use them by some perceived similarity between laboratory tasks and situations at home. Normally, parents do give infants explicit instruction for going down household stairs. However, in the current study, families refrained from teaching babies how to descend stairs. Although most infants who learned to descend furniture were taught the backing position by their parents, there was no evidence that the backing method transferred from furniture to slopes. Moreover, it is unlikely that parents coached infants to hesitate, look, probe unfamiliar surfaces with their hands and feet, or explore new locomotor methods by shifting positions.

Aversive Consequences

Although infants eventually avoid aversive situations, there was no evidence that aversive consequences were the impetus for change or that infants required feedback from errors on slopes. Most parents reported in their diaries that infants fell frequently while walking or crawling around the home. However, these were minor incidents, and the infants were not injured. One infant did experience a serious fall, but the incident had no bearing on his performance on slopes. No-transfer infant E-10 fell headfirst down a flight of stairs while traveling around in a mechanical baby-walker 4 days before crawling onset and was rushed to the emergency room with contusions on his face. At his first test session a few days later, he went headfirst down risky slopes in the laboratory task. Similarly, cross-sectional samples showed no effects on slopes due to serious falls (broken legs, stitches) at home (Adolph, 1995). Babies simply dragged their casts and bandages over the brink with the rest of the children. Likewise, there is no evidence that serious falls at home spur avoidance behavior on the visual cliff (Scarr & Salapatek, 1970).

Moreover, the data indicate that occasional falls down laboratory slopes did not spur learning, although infants often behaved as though falling downhill were aversive by fussing and asking for their mother. Within sessions, after falling on one slope, infants were most likely to attempt the same crawling or walking response on the same hill at the very next trial. When infants slid down hills or avoided going, they refused outright after a successful trial on a shallower slope. Control-group infants behaved similarly to experimental-group infants, although the control-group infants had far less experience on slopes; age-matched controls with no prior experience on laboratory slopes behaved similarly to the experimental-group infants in the current study. Likewise, recent research in the cognitive literature indicates that children may discover new strategies and solutions without receiving feedback from errors. Preschool children, for example, were just as likely to discover new, more efficient counting procedures after successful solutions as they were after getting the wrong answer (e.g., Siegler & Jenkins, 1989).

In fact, the whole notion of error-driven learning may be a red herring in this case. Adaptive locomotion in risky situations requires immediate recognition of a problem a few steps ahead, not after the fact. In the slope task, adaptive go ratios meant that infants recognized risky hills *before* they attempted to go, rather than after receiving feedback from the consequences of mistakes or correct solutions.

Serendipitous Discovery Instigated by Biomechanical Factors

A third way for infants to discover new movements is by accident. Useful, new exploratory movements and locomotor methods could emerge serendipitously from the confluence of infants' growing bodies, their changing locomotor proficiency, and the biomechanical constraints imposed by properties of the ground surface. (Thelen & Smith, 1994, and Thelen & Ulrich, 1991, propose a similar explanation for the emergence of new motor patterns.) Discovery is not left entirely to chance because infants must be in the right place at the right time. However, discovery does not require deliberate forethought, only that infants recognize a good thing once they have got it. The subsequent learning process would involve the selection and honing of movements already present.

Emergence of Visual and Haptic Exploration in Crawling

Effects of poor crawling proficiency may explain infants' high levels of prolonged looking and touching in their first weeks of crawling on both uphill and downhill slopes and on both safe and risky ones (see Figure 23*b*). Beginning crawlers' visual and haptic exploration may not have been deliberate. On some trials, poor crawling proficiency may have spurred useful, new exploratory movements that generated information pertinent to coping with risky ground.

In their first weeks of crawling, most infants are weak, top-heavy, and poorly proficient. New crawlers, especially belly crawlers, have highly variable crawling movements, and variability shows no decrease over weeks of belly crawling (Freedland & Bertenthal, 1994; Vereijken et al., 1995). Owing to difficulty in the sheer biomechanics of struggling forward, beginning crawlers often execute the same exploratory looking and touching movements crawling on flat ground as they use to explore slopes, cliffs, or waterbeds. Infants' heavy heads keep their eyes pointed toward the ground, ensuring that they take a long look at the ground beneath their hands. Every few steps, even on safe, flat ground, infants pause, pat the floor, and rock back and forth over their wrists, as though gathering energy for the next burst of crawling steps (e.g., Goldfield, 1993). Infants' weak arms keep body weight distributed back toward the legs from step to step, with the result that as they hobble along, patting, rocking, and resting, beginning crawlers inadvertently may put their hands on the edge of a novel surface, sway to and fro, and generate torques around their wrists.

In other words, beginning crawlers may initially execute exploratory movements without understanding their relevance for guiding locomotion. In the current study, when beginning crawlers paused on the starting platform, it counted toward latency and looking. When they stopped, patted, and rocked at the edge of a slope, it counted toward touching. Regardless of beginning crawlers' intentions, serendipitous exploratory movements can give rise to information about properties of the ground surface necessary for balance control from the start of independent mobility. More important, experienced crawlers' deliberate exploration in later sessions used the same looking, swaying, and touching movements that infants had demonstrated earlier on.

Perceptual Novelty and Poor Crawling Proficiency

Poor crawling proficiency may also account for the earlier appearance of adaptive responding on the visual cliff than on slopes and for infants' differential rates of looking and touching on risky and safe downhill slopes in their first weeks of crawling. Serendipitous looking at the ground surface provides infants with extensive opportunities to learn that everyday terrain has continuous visible texture. Although both cliffs and slopes present comparable disparity in depth between starting and landing platforms, the visual cliff has an abrupt discontinuity in visible texture, whereas slopes provide continuous visible texture along the path. If tested on steeper slopes ($>40°$) more closely approximating the sheer drop-off on a visual cliff, young crawlers may show earlier adaptive responses.

Serendipitous looking at the ground may also provide beginning crawlers with experience seeing everyday ground surfaces close to infants' eyes. Typically, furniture and other obstructions in the path are also close to infants' head and eyes. An abrupt discontinuity in visible texture or a steep hill slanting away from infants' eyes may be perceptually novel. The novelty of cliffs or steep, risky slopes may have prompted infants to engage in prolonged looking and touching, without initial knowledge that the surfaces were risky for locomotion.

Attention to information about a continuous surface that is pertinent to balance control may appear later than attention to information about a discontinuity in the path because crawling is remarkably stable. During belly crawling, for example, the abdomen rests on the floor during part of each crawling cycle. On their hands and knees, infants can execute exploratory patting and rocking movements without shifting their entire weight over the brink of a risky surface. The stability of infants' quadruped posture means that there is no pressing urgency for beginning crawlers to attend to information about everyday flat surfaces that is pertinent to balance control. Differentiation can await improvements in crawling proficiency and the refinement of exploratory movements. Accordingly, adaptive responses on slopes and waterbeds appear later developmentally than avoidance on the visual cliff.

Consequences of Poor Walking Proficiency for Visual and Haptic Exploration

Biomechanical constraints may also explain the lower levels of prolonged looking and touching in infants' first weeks of walking than in their first weeks of crawling found in the current research (see Figure 23*b*) and in previous cross-sectional work (Adolph et al., 1993a). In contrast to crawling, poor walking proficiency may work against serendipitous learning in a safe arena. Deficiencies in early walking gait result from poor balance control during periods of single-limb support (e.g., Breniere & Bril, 1988; Bril & Breniere, 1992a). New walkers' entire weight shifts over their leading leg with each step, and infants therefore put their moving leg down as quickly as possible so that they do not fall over. This means that, unlike when crawling, when walking, there is no serendipitously safe halt in forward momentum at the edge of a risky surface. If new walkers do not detect visual information specifying loss of balance, they are likely to step over the brink of a risky hill or onto the edge of an impossibly slippery or pliant surface.

In addition, upright posture is unstable compared with crawling, and walking is more easily disrupted by visual and mechanical perturbations of balance. New walkers, for example, topple over in a moving room (e.g., Stoffregen et al., 1987). Although manifold visual and mechanical information is available to specify new walkers' precarious balance, infants may have difficulty obtaining it. New walkers' problems keeping balance may hamper them from orienting their head and eyes toward the ground beneath their feet. In contrast to crawling, where the head naturally points downward and infants have to work against gravity to lift it, in upright locomotion the natural position for the head and eyes is straight ahead. In fact, rotating the head downward shifts infants' center of mass forward, resulting in even more jeopardized balance. The problem is similar for novice adults wearing ice skates or stilts. We freeze degrees of freedom to maintain balance by keeping our heads stiffly positioned upright above the shoulder girdle (e.g., Vereijken, van Emmerick, Whiting, & Newell, 1993). On slopes, new walkers had a "Frankenstein" gait, with arms held up, legs stiff, and head pointing straight ahead, as they walked over the brink of risky hills. In fact, even experienced walkers may have had difficulty keeping upright balance while executing exploratory movements. Many experienced walkers held the corner posts at the top of slopes while peering downward or touching hills with their feet, as though requiring additional support to keep their balance. In contrast, only one crawler on only one trial held a post for support.

Ironically, despite poor walking proficiency, infants appear determined to try their new, upright method of locomotion. In the current study, infants preferred to judge possibilities for locomotion relative to their new, more grown-up posture. When the experimenter started new walkers in a prone position, infants often stood themselves up and faced slopes from their new upright position, preferring to be hapless walkers rather than proficient crawlers.

Skilled Locomotion and the Emergence of New Descent Methods

Some potentially beneficial effects of excellent locomotor proficiency are straightforward. For example, good crawling and walking skills may lead to refinements in exploratory movements and may free up attentional resources for opportunities to execute them. Strong correlations between measures of crawling proficiency and go ratios at infants' final crawling session are consistent with this account. Likewise, better differentiation of optic flow in older, more experienced infants may have resulted from improvements in walking proficiency (Stoffregen et al., 1987). In addition, highly proficient crawlers and walkers may be more motivated than beginners to optimize energy expenditure by minimizing the length of their path in detour tasks. More proficient infants may have more wherewithal to execute subtle shifts in posture in order to cope with obstacles and apertures (e.g., Palmer, 1987).

In addition, proficient locomotion may lead to less obvious benefits. Good skill invites a different kind of variability by introducing infants to propitious, new situations. Like exploratory movements, new locomotor methods may emerge spontaneously in the context of doing something else.

For example, in the current study, 13 experimental-group infants may have discovered backing and sitting methods serendipitously in the course of trying to crawl down steep slopes (Wechsler, 1995; Wechsler & Adolph, 1995). As infants' bodies became more maturely proportioned, and as their crawling proficiency improved, they spent more trials on steep slopes. As infants attempted to crawl down steep slopes, keeping their arms stiffly extended in front and their legs tightly flexed beneath their rumps to prevent falling, gravity gradually pulled their legs around until they found themselves sliding down sideways or rotating 180° in a backing position. Some infants said "Uh oh" or "Oh no," and several of them crawled back up to the starting platform and looked down the hill in puzzlement. After one or more accidental backing trials, infants executed the backing method deliberately before leaving the starting platform. After experiencing the backing position mid-slope, some infants continued to test various components of backing on the starting platform, and others, like Kohler's (1925) insightful chimps, stared down the hill, then smoothly switched into a backing position and slid down. McGraw (1935) observed a similar serendipitous discovery process for the backing position in one child receiving daily practice descending slopes.

Likewise, control-group infant C-13 provided a striking case of the serendipitous discovery of sitting. In her tenth week of crawling, she attempted to crawl down a 28° slope. Her arms were extended in front, and, with each cycle, her legs became more and more straddled to the sides. To prevent herself from falling she pushed hard with her arms and found herself perched in a straddle split. With additional pushes, she achieved a sitting position and slid safely down. This scenario was repeated three times within the single test session.

Summary: Impetus for Change

Infants do not require an explicit or aversive impetus for change. Rather, the raw materials for a differentiation/selection process may arise from biomechanical and situational factors that introduce variability into the system at opportune times. The most optimal developmental conditions for the emergence of exploratory movements may be a fat, weak body and an extended period of belly crawling. The most optimal conditions for the emergence of alternative locomotor methods may be a more maturely proportioned, strong body and an extended period of crawling on hands and knees.

It is important to note that these examples of serendipitous discovery are not the result of random thrashing or trial-and-error learning. But, when they first appeared, neither were behaviors executed with deliberate forethought. Instead, infants' repertoires of exploratory movements and locomotor methods may emerge spontaneously in the context of a goal-directed task. Like cases of exaptation in evolutionary development, infants were trying to do one thing and found themselves doing something else that turned out to be extremely useful. Infants learn to recognize the functional relevance of new movements over many weeks of crawling and walking.

WHAT INFANTS LEARN FROM EVERYDAY EXPERIENCE

Despite evidence linking everyday locomotor experience with adaptive responding in a variety of locomotor tasks (slopes, cliffs, apertures/obstacles, moving rooms/floors, stairs), to date, researchers know little about what infants learn from everyday experience. The detailed observations of learning and transfer in the current study provided a unique opportunity to examine the content of infants' knowledge. As described below, the data indicate that infants need not learn particular facts, concepts, or simple associative responses. Rather, results suggest that infants learn general purpose exploratory movements for discriminating safe from risky ground and more special purpose locomotor methods for traversing risky ground.

Rescue

Infants did not learn to rely on a stalwart adult to rescue them. The experimenter rescued infants on every downhill trial when they began to fall, and most experimental-group infants experienced dozens of rescues. Similarly, vigilant parents rescue their infants from potentially perilous consequences in everyday situations. However, in the slope task, infants became more cautious rather than more reckless with weeks of experience. Likewise, parents withdraw support by providing infants with increased access to such potentially risky situations as going down household stairs and furniture.

Knowledge about Surface Properties

Surprisingly, results indicate that the crucial content of learning was not knowledge about slopes per se or, for that matter, knowledge about Plexiglas-covered cliffs, waterbeds, oiled plastic, or whatever other novel surface was used to test infants in the laboratory. Few infants have experience with such novel surface properties prior to exposure in the laboratory. In the present study, experimental- and control-group infants showed similar slope boundaries, go ratios, and exploratory procedures at each of the matched sessions, and neither group had exposure to slopes at home (see Figures 9, 11, 14, and 18 above). Infants in cross-sectional slopes studies with approximately the same age and locomotor experience behaved similarly to infants in the current study without prior experience on slopes (Adolph, 1995; Adolph et al., 1993a). Controls in a cross-sectional study showed patterns of avoidance that were similar to those exhibited by infants in a longitudinal study with bimonthly exposure (Campos et al., 1978).

Simple Associations

Most important for understanding adaptive locomotion, the data from this study indicate that infants do not learn to pair a static concept of their own abilities with a particular surface property or to pair a particular surface property with a particular locomotor response. In fact, such simple associative learning would be maladaptive because infants' bodies and skills change from

123

week to week and the everyday terrain is changeable. Chunky babies become slimmer, and small babies get larger (see Figure 20 above). Slow, plodding crawlers one week become fast, efficient crawlers the next, expert crawlers become unstable walkers, and so on (see Figure 19 above). Accordingly, slope boundaries changed from week to week, and infants' go ratios showed corresponding change (see Figures 9 and 11 above). Apparently, infants learned to detect ongoing changes in their own crawling and walking proficiency and to relate properties of their bodies to the properties of the current ground surface.

However, it is important to note that the ordinal nature of slope groups used to interpret go ratios (+5°, +13° and +18°) is confounded with *absolute degree of slant*. That is, within sessions, hills in the +18° range are always steeper than hills in the +13° range and the +5° range of slopes. Thus, across sessions, if slope boundaries increase steadily, then hills that were previously in the +18° range will be grouped in the +13° or +5° range in subsequent sessions. This point is important because it raises an alternative explanation for the decrease in children's go ratios over weeks of crawling and walking: perhaps children did not select locomotor responses relative to their current level of proficiency but rather simply learned to associate sliding with the steepest degrees of slant. According to this explanation, locomotor experience led to refusals on extremely steep hills rather than to relative judgments because progressive change in the absolute degree of slant included in the +5°, +13°, and +18° ranges of slopes led to "smarter" go ratios.

However, there are several sources of evidence that belie this alternative explanation. First, after they began crawling on their hands and knees, six experimental-group infants slid down extremely steep hills that they had crawled safely down in previous weeks as belly crawlers. If they had simply paired 36°, for example, with its consequences for locomotion, they should have attempted to crawl rather than refusing this slope outright. Second, nine experimental-group infants refused to crawl down demonstrably safe hills in the intermediate range of slopes (e.g., 10°–30°) after crawling down them successfully week after week in previous sessions. Overly cautious responding should not result from associative pairing between absolute degree of slant and a particular locomotor response.

Third, this alternative explanation is hard-pressed to account for lack of transfer from crawling to walking, lack of transfer from prone to standing positions on consecutive trials, and lack of transfer from falling on one trial to falling on the next trial at the very same slope in the very same position. That is, if children simply learned to associate particular responses with absolute degree of slope, then they should have learned to attempt shallow hills and slide down steep hills regardless of changes in locomotor proficiency, changes in typical method of locomotion, and changes in vantage point. Fourth, in an earlier cross-sectional study with 14-month-old walkers

THE DEVELOPMENT OF INFANT LOCOMOTION

(Adolph, 1995), go ratios were also calculated relative to each infant's slope boundaries. In that study, downhill slope boundaries ranged from 6° to 28°. Go ratios were scaled closely to infants' slope boundaries rather than to absolute degree of slant. In other words, infants with shallow boundaries were more likely to refuse 36° than infants with steep slope boundaries.

General Purpose Exploratory Movements

What is required to discriminate safe from risky ground may be simply possessing both a repertoire of exploratory movements and the ability to interpret the information gleaned from those movements in terms of balance control. These exploratory movements must be general and flexible enough to allow infants to predict whether they can maintain their balance from step to step. Exploration must take into account the changeable nature of everyday terrain and the changing constraints of infants' own bodies and skills. Looking, swaying, and touching movements yield multimodal and redundant information about whether the ground will allow infants to maintain their balance in their current posture. Exploratory shifts in position generate information that is relevant to maintaining balance while engaged in a variety of locomotor methods.

In particular, detecting threats to balance control requires information about the limits of permissible postural sway (Stoffregen et al., in press). Infants will lose their balance if their body moves beyond their base of support and they do not have sufficient muscle strength and coordination to pull themselves back into position. When the ground is too sloping, too slippery, or too pliant, infants must reduce their angle of body rotation by stiffening and locking their joints, modifying ongoing gait patterns, or switching to a different method of locomotion (e.g., Adolph, Gill, et al., 1996).

Results suggest that infants may learn to detect information relevant to balance control posture by posture, rather than surface by surface or task by task. Apparently, the generalized context of everyday locomotion ensures that information obtained from exploratory looking and touching movements transfers to new ground surfaces and to changes in infants' body dimensions or locomotor proficiency. During the course of everyday locomotion, infants are exposed to a variety of surfaces varying in path size, rigidity, friction, etc.—kitchen linoleum, bathroom tile, throw rugs and hardwood floors, playpen and bed mattresses, grass, sand, and so on—and they steer between obstacles, over and under toys and furniture, and up and down stairs. Presumably, infants spend several hours each day crawling or walking around their homes. By the time infants exhibit adaptive responses on a visual cliff or on slopes, they have experienced thousands of "trials" viewing and touching everyday ground surfaces and observing the consequences for balance control.

Everyday practice maintaining balance in a crawling position, for example, may help infants learn how fast and how far their bodies can rotate as they rock back and forth over their wrists and how much muscle force they can generate to counter rotational forces. Transfer from such home experience to novel lab tasks may be facilitated by the massive exposure afforded by and the generalized context of everyday locomotion.

However, everyday locomotion does not facilitate transfer to unfamiliar postures and vantage points. In a new upright position, balance requirements are different, and old exploratory movements may be difficult to execute and less informative. Walking infants' bodies sway around the hips or ankles rather than the wrists, compensatory muscle responses are generated primarily in leg or back muscles instead of the upper body, and the base of support is reduced to the smaller space between infants' feet. An analogous situation for adults occurs when we drive a new vehicle. We display rapid, positive transfer when we drive a rental car of a different model and of different dimensions than our own. We quickly adjust the seat and rearview mirror, test the brakes, get the feel of the steering wheel, and drive off smoothly without mishap. However, imagine sitting for the first time in the cab of a tractor-trailer. The mechanics of driving are very different (there are more gears and devices), and we face the road from a new, higher vantage point. Our old exploratory procedures may no longer yield the same information, and we may indeed have trouble gauging our speed, staying in one lane, parallel parking, and distinguishing safe from risky maneuvers.

Special Purpose Locomotor Methods

When infants' typical method of locomotion is impossible, they must select an alternative method for traversing risky ground. A second kind of knowledge that infants bring to each locomotor task is a repertoire of locomotor methods—their typical crawling and walking gaits as well as more specialized methods, such as climbing, sliding, scooting, stooping, and so on, for coping with more unusual tasks.

On downhill slopes, special purpose methods were not fixed routines. Infants continually discovered new descent methods (see Figure 17 above), and variety in locomotor methods was consistently high across weeks of testing (see Figure 16 above) and within sessions. Likewise, in several studies, some infants concocted multiple solutions in tasks where the experimenters had foreseen only one solution. For example, infants deployed tricky detours to escape impossibly steep uphill slopes (in the current study), they detoured along the edge of the visual cliff (Campos et al., 1978), and they displayed multiple maneuvers in a stair-climbing task (Ulrich et al., 1990).

Compared with generalized exploratory movements, special purpose lo-

126

comotor methods appear more tied to the environmental contexts in which they are acquired. Although most infants eventually used the backing position to descend household furniture, home stairs, lab stairs, and lab slopes, the method appeared in different tasks at different, widely spaced times. There was no evidence of immediate or automatic transfer across tasks. In contrast, special purpose methods are not posture specific. Infants did not forget various sliding positions over the transition from crawling to walking. Rather, the use of old descent methods awaited differentiation of safe from risky hills.

Why might home experience facilitate transfer of exploratory movements but not special purpose methods? Specialized forms of locomotion are used less frequently and are limited to a narrower range of everyday situations—going up and down stairs, furniture, and playground equipment. In contrast to the hundreds of hours that infants accumulate crawling and walking over various flat surfaces at home, their experience with special purpose methods of locomotion is quite limited. Parents closely monitor infants' use of special purpose skills and typically coach them to use particular solutions. Learning may be more context bound when experience is infrequent and limited to practice exercising only one type of locomotor method or executing only one type of solution. Thus, learning to judge possibilities for crawling or walking over stairs, for example, may transfer to slopes, but the particular locomotor response may not.

LEARNING TO MAKE ON-LINE DECISIONS

In the end, adaptive locomotion requires infants to make on-line decisions. The end product of development is the ability to learn on-line, from moment to moment and from step to step—a kind of learning to learn. Over weeks of crawling and walking, infants acquire an arsenal of increasingly effective exploratory movements for obtaining information on-line as they face each new surface from the starting platform. Figure 23d above illustrates a schematic account of how infants may obtain on-line the information required for deciding how to navigate the ground ahead. Each step in this schematic is marked by additional sources of information available to infants as they decide whether to continue with their typical method of locomotion or select an alternative locomotor response. Figure 23a–c summarizes the developmental progression for each aspect of on-line decision making.

First, infants take a *quick glance* at the surface of support. If the ground looks safe, they plunge ahead without modifying their ongoing method of locomotion. This glance-and-plunge tactic is optimal when the consequences of falling are trivial because learning by doing yields the maximum amount of information in the shortest amount of time. In the slopes task, trials began only after infants made visual contact with the landing platform. Virtually

127

every uphill trial and more than half the downhill trials had latencies of less than 1 second. This means that infants had decided on a locomotor method in the few moments that it took for the experimenter to lower them toward the starting platform and for them to glance at the hill and take a step or two. Sometimes infants chose their typical method of locomotion, and sometimes they chose an alternative method. The functional outcome of quick glances improved dramatically over weeks of experience. Important sources of information may be the distance of the surface from infants' eyes, the angle of the slope relative to the plane of gaze, or visual/proprioceptive information resulting from infants' first step or two on the starting platform.

Second, if a quick glance hints at something amiss, infants may pause on the patch of starting ground and take a *longer look*. Presumably, prolonged visual exploration is accompanied by stepping, swaying, and looking movements executed with the eyes, head, and body. These movements generate visual and mechanical information relevant to balance control (e.g., Lee, 1994; Mark et al., 1990) as well as visual information about the properties of the ground ahead. If prolonged looking and swaying movements indicate safe going, then infants continue along the path with their typical method of locomotion. On slopes, infants usually maintained an orientation toward the landing platform during the time that they hesitated. Across sessions, long looks were followed by infants' typical method and alternative locomotor methods in approximately equal proportions, and the functional outcome of long looks improved with weeks of experience.

Third, if a long look or tipsy sway suggests a risky proposition, infants can obtain additional information from *coordinated looking and touching*. They probe the surface with their hands and feet, all the while looking at their limbs and the ground. If the touch specifies adequate support for maintaining balance, infants continue with their typical method of locomotion. On slopes, detailed coding of infants' touches showed that infants hesitated for several seconds prior to their first touch, suggesting that visual information obtained from a long look prompted the touch. Infants executed a variety of touching movements with their hands and feet—usually stepping and rocking movements at the brink of the hill. Touching yields information about slant, friction, and rigidity by generating torque at the wrists or ankles and shearing forces between the extremity and the surface. Sometimes touches were followed by use of infants' typical method and sometimes by an alternative method.

Finally, if a touch suggests danger from falling, children *explore alternative locomotor methods* and test them out before going. Means-ends exploration functions to generate information pertinent to less practiced forms of locomotion, such as the various sliding positions for going down hills. If infants discover an appropriate alternative, they use it. If not, they stay put and await retrieval by a caregiver. On slopes, shifts in position were nearly always followed by refusals, indicating that infants had already decided that slopes were risky. Over weeks of crawling, avoidance responses were replaced by sliding positions.

SUMMARY

The four-phase decision-making process outlined above is not a rigid program that infants follow in an unvarying temporal order. Children's behavior in every study was much more flexible than that. Sometimes infants proceed straight from a quick glance to touching, means-ends shifts in position, or refusal, and sometimes they cycle through various procedures, such as touching, then testing a few positions, then touching some more. However, the data from the current study and previous ones are consistent with these types of exploration, each of them turning up multimodal and redundant information and occurring in a loose temporal order. In particular, the procedure in the current study ensured that each trial began with a quick glance. Detailed sequential coding of infants' touches showed prolonged looking prior to the first touch. And most shifts in position were followed by a sliding position for descent.

Moreover, each phase in the schematic is itself an example of differentiation and selection over developmental time. It takes many weeks before infants benefit from a quick glance, long look, or touch and many weeks before infants perform means-ends behaviors. Together, the four phases exemplify a continual process of generating information, differentiating requisite structures, and selecting adaptive responses in turn. Most important, the schematic illustrates the information-gathering aspect of navigating the everyday environment. Adaptive locomotion requires movement—both exploratory movements to obtain information and performatory movements to make use of it.

Future Directions

In sum, this *Monograph* points to several useful directions for further research on infant locomotion. First, to understand how ongoing movements are adapted to change in local conditions, we must establish the kinds of information that infants detect at various points in development and document corresponding changes in exploratory activity and locomotor responses. As information becomes differentiated, infants' responses become better adapted to task constraints. Because learning is related to ongoing developmental changes (bodies, skills, and experience), it is important to chart the path of learning longitudinally, especially over transitions in posture. Second, to understand how infants deploy a variety of flexible responses, we must observe the acquisition process firsthand. In particular, focus on processes that promote variability in children's repertoires may yield useful insights into mechanisms of change. Third, understanding transfer from one locomotor task to another requires careful experimental manipulations of the context within which infants solve various locomotor problems. Presumably, varied or extensive experience may aid discovery of relevant similarities between the old task and the new. The current study provides a first step in these directions.

REFERENCES

Acredolo, L. P. (1988). Infant mobility and spatial development. In J. Stiles-Davis, M. Kritchevsky, & U. Bellugi (Eds.), *Spatial cognition: Brain bases and development*. Hillsdale, NJ: Erlbaum.

Acredolo, L. P., Adams, A., & Goodwyn, S. W. (1984). The role of self-produced movement and visual tracking in infant spatial orientation. *Journal of Experimental Child Psychology, 38,* 312–317.

Adolph, K. E. (1995). A psychophysical assessment of toddlers' ability to cope with slopes. *Journal of Experimental Psychology: Human Perception and Performance, 21,* 734–750.

Adolph, K. E., Eppler, M. A., & Gibson, E. J. (1993a). Crawling versus walking infants' perception of affordances for locomotion over sloping surfaces. *Child Development, 64,* 1158–1174.

Adolph, K. E., Eppler, M. A., & Gibson, E. J. (1993b). Development of perception of affordances. In C. Rovee-Collier & L. P. Lipsitt (Eds.), *Advances in infancy research* (Vol. **8**). Norwood, NJ: Ablex.

Adolph, K. E., Gill, S., Lucero, A., & Fadl, Y. (1996, April). *Emergence of a stepping strategy: How infants learn to walk down slopes.* Poster presented at the International Conference on Infant Studies, Providence, RI.

Adolph, K. E., & Pursifull, S. (1993, August). *Changing perspectives from crawling to walking: Position-specific learning in infants descending slopes.* Poster presented at the International Conference on Event Perception and Action, Vancouver.

Adolph, K. E., Ruff, H. A., Cappozoli, M. C., & Kim, D. R. (1994, November). *Preschoolers' strategies for allocating attention: Individual differences and task constraints.* Poster presented at the meeting of the Psychonomic Society, St. Louis.

Adolph, K. E., Vereijken, B., Byrne, K. J., Urspruch, T., Ilustre, I., & Ondrako, A. M. (1996, April). *Footprint method of gait analysis: New insights into infant walking.* Poster presented at the International Conference on Infant Studies, Providence, RI.

Ashmead, D. H., & McCarty, M. E. (1991). Postural sway of human infants while standing in light and dark. *Child Development, 62,* 1276–1287.

Atkinson, J., Hood, B., Wattam-Bell, J., Anker, S., & Tricklebank, J. (1988). Development of orientation discrimination in infancy. *Perception, 17,* 587–595.

Avolio, A. M., Thompson, B. E., Lin, H. R., Biswas, S., & Arnet, H. S. (1997, April). *Adaptive action in infants: Psychophysical double staircase procedure.* Poster presented at the meeting of the Society for Research in Child Development, Washington, DC.

Bai, D. L., & Bertenthal, B. I. (1992). Locomotor status and the development of spatial search skills. *Child Development, 63,* 215–226.

Behrman, R. E. (1992). *Nelson textbook of pediatrics.* Philadelphia: W. B. Saunders.

131

Benson, J. B., & Uzgiris, I. C. (1985). Effect of self-initiated locomotion on infant search activity. *Developmental Psychology,* **21**(6), 923–931.

Bernstein, N. (1967). *The co-ordination and regulation of movements.* Oxford: Pergamon.

Bertenthal, B. I., & Bai, D. L. (1989). Infants' sensitivity to optical flow for controlling posture. *Developmental Psychology,* **25,** 936–945.

Bertenthal, B. I., & Campos, J. J. (1984). A reexamination of fear and its determinants on the visual cliff. *Psychophysiology,* **21**(4), 413–417.

Bertenthal, B. I., & Campos, J. J. (1987). New directions in the study of early experience. *Child Development,* **58,** 560–567.

Bertenthal, B. I., & Campos, J. J. (1990). A systems approach to the organizing effects of self-produced locomotion during infancy. In C. Rovee-Collier & L. P. Lipsitt (Eds.), *Advances in infancy research* (Vol. **6**). Norwood, NJ: Ablex.

Bertenthal, B. I., Campos, J. J., & Barrett, K. C. (1984). Self-produced locomotion: An organizer of emotional, cognitive, and social development in infancy. In R. N. Emde & R. J. Harmon (Eds.), *Continuities and discontinuities in development.* New York: Plenum.

Bertenthal, B. I., & Clifton, R. (in press). Perception and action. In D. Kuhn & R. Siegler (Eds.), *Handbook of child psychology: Cognition, perception, and language* (Vol. **2**). New York: Wiley.

Biringen, Z., Emde, R. N., Campos, J. J., & Appelbaum, M. I. (1995). Affective reorganization in the infant, the mother, and the dyad: The role of upright locomotion and its timing. *Child Development,* **66,** 499–514.

Boening, D. D. (1977). Evaluation of a clinical method of gait analysis. *Physical Therapy,* **57**(7), 795–798.

Breniere, Y., & Bril, B. (1988). Pourquoi les enfants marchent en tombant alors que les adultes tombent en marchant? [Why does the child walk in falling whereas the adult falls in walking?]. *Comptes Rendus* (Academy of Science, Paris), **307,** 617–622.

Breniere, Y., Bril, B., & Fontaine, R. (1989). Analysis of the transition from upright stance to steady state locomotion in children with under 200 days of autonomous walking. *Journal of Motor Behavior,* **21**(1), 20–37.

Bril, B., & Breniere, Y. (1989). Steady-state velocity and temporal structure of gait during the first six months of autonomous walking. *Human Movement Science,* **8,** 99–122.

Bril, B., & Breniere, Y. (1991). Timing invariances in toddlers' gait. In J. Fagard & P. Wolff (Eds.), *The development of timing control and temporal organization in coordinated action* (Advances in Psychology Series). Amsterdam: Elsevier.

Bril, B., & Breniere, Y. (1992a). Postural requirements and progression velocity in young walkers. *Journal of Motor Behavior,* **24,** 105–116.

Bril, B., & Breniere, Y. (1992b). Posture and independent locomotion in early childhood: Learning to walk or learning dynamic postural control? In G. J. P. Salvelsbergh (Ed.), *The development of coordination in infancy.* Amsterdam: North-Holland/Elsevier.

Burnett, C. N., & Johnson, E. W. (1971). Development of gait in childhood: Part 2. *Developmental Medicine and Child Neurology,* **13,** 207–215.

Burnside, L. H. (1927). Coordination in the locomotion of infants. *Genetic Psychology Monographs,* **2,** 279–372.

Burton, A. W., Pick, H. L., Heinrichs, M., & Greer, N. L. (1989, April). *To go over or under.* Poster presented at the meeting of the Society for Research in Child Development, Kansas City, MO.

Butterworth, G., & Cicchetti, A. (1978). Visual calibration of posture in normal and motor retarded Down's syndrome infants. *Perception,* **7,** 513–525.

Butterworth, G., & Hicks, L. (1977). Visual proprioception and postural stability in infancy: A developmental study. *Perception,* **6,** 255–262.

Butterworth, G., & Pope, M. (1983). Origine et fonction de la proprioception visuelle chez l'enfant. In S. de Schonen (Ed.), *Le developpement dans la premiere anee*. Paris: Presses Universitaires de France.

Campos, J. J., & Bertenthal, B. I. (1984). The importance of self-produced locomotion in infancy. *Infant Mental Health Journal*, **5**(3), 160–171.

Campos, J. J., Bertenthal, B. I., & Kermoian, R. (1992). Early experience and emotional development: The emergence of wariness of heights. *Psychological Science*, **3**(1), 61–64.

Campos, J., Hiatt, S., Ramsay, D., Henderson, C., & Svejda, M. (1978). The emergence of fear on the visual cliff. In M. Lewis & L. Rosenblum (Eds.), *The development of affect*. New York: Plenum.

Carello, C., Fitzpatrick, P., Domaniewicz, I., Chan, T. C., & Turvey, M. T. (1992). Effortful touch with minimal movement. *Journal of Experimental Psychology: Human Perception and Performance*, **18**, 290–302.

Carrol, J. J., & Gibson, E. J. (1981, April). *Differentiation of an aperture from an obstacle under conditions of motion by three-month-old infants*. Paper presented at the meeting of the Society for Research in Child Development, Boston.

Clark, J. E., & Phillips, S. J. (1987). The step cycle organization of infant walkers. *Journal of Motor Behavior*, **19**, 412–433.

Clark, J. E., Whitall, J., & Phillips, S. J. (1988). Human interlimb coordination: The first 6 months of independent walking. *Developmental Psychobiology*, **21**(5), 445–456.

Cornsweet, T. N. (1962). The staircase-method in psychophysics. *American Journal of Psychology*, **75**, 485–491.

Dean, G. A. (1965). An analysis of the energy expenditure in level and grade walking. *Ergonomics*, **8**, 31–47.

Diamond, A. (1990a). The development and neural bases of memory functions as indexed by the A-not-B error and delayed response tasks in human infants and infant monkeys. In A. Diamond (Ed.), *The development and neural bases of higher cognitive functions*. New York: New York Academy of Sciences.

Diamond, A. (1990b). Developmental time course in human infants and infant monkeys, and the neural bases of inhibitory control in reaching. In A. Diamond (Ed.), *The development and neural bases of higher cognitive functions*. New York: New York Academy of Sciences.

Eppler, M. A. (1995). Development of manipulatory skills and the deployment of attention. *Infant Behavior and Development*, **18**, 391–405.

Eppler, M. A., Adolph, K. E., & Weiner, T. (1996). The developmental relationship between infants' exploration and action on sloping surfaces. *Infant Behavior and Development*, **19**, 259–264.

Fitzpatrick, P., Carello, C., Schmidt, R. C., & Corey, D. (1994). Haptic and visual perception of an affordance for upright posture. *Ecological Psychology*, **6**, 265–287.

Forssberg, H., & Nashner, L. M. (1982). Ontogenetic development of postural control in man: Adaptation to altered support and visual conditions during stance. *Journal of Neuroscience*, **2**, 545–552.

Frankenburg, W. K., & Dodds, J. B. (1967). The Denver developmental screening test. *Journal of Pediatrics*, **71**, 181–191.

Freedland, R. L., & Bertenthal, B. I. (1994). Developmental changes in interlimb coordination: Transition to hands-and-knees crawling. *Psychological Science*, **5**, 26–32.

Gesell, A. (1946). The ontogenesis of infant behavior. In L. Carmichael (Ed.), *Manual of child psychology* (1st ed.). New York: Wiley.

Gesell, A. (1954). Maturation and the patterning of behavior. In L. Carmichael (Ed.), *Manual of child psychology* (2d ed.). New York: Wiley.

Gesell, A., & Ames, L. B. (1940). The ontogenetic organization of prone behavior in human infancy. *Journal of Genetic Psychology*, **56**, 247–263.

Gesell, A., & Thompson, H. (1938). *The psychology of early growth including norms of infant behavior and a method of genetic analysis.* New York: Macmillan.

Giacalone, W. R., & Rarick, G. L. (1985). Dynamic balance of preschool children as reflected by performance on beam-walking tasks. *Journal of Genetic Psychology,* **146,** 307–318.

Gibson, E. J. (1969). *Principles of perceptual learning and development.* New York: Appleton-Century-Crofts.

Gibson, E. J. (1988). Exploratory behavior in the development of perceiving, acting and the acquiring of knowledge. *Annual Review of Psychology,* **39,** 1–41.

Gibson, E. J. (1991). Prospects for a new approach to perceptual learning. In E. J. Gibson (Ed.), *An odyssey in learning and perception.* Cambridge, MA: MIT Press.

Gibson, E. J. (1994a, September). *An ecological psychologist's prolegomena for perceptual development: A functional approach.* Paper presented at the meeting of the International Society for Ecological Psychology, Storrs, CT.

Gibson, E. J. (1994b). Has psychology a future? *Psychological Science,* **5,** 69–76.

Gibson, E. J., & Olum, V. (1960). Experimental methods of studying perception in children. In P. H. Mussen (Ed.), *Handbook of research methods in child development.* New York: Wiley.

Gibson, E. J., Riccio, G., Schmuckler, M. A., Stoffregen, T. A., Rosenberg, D., & Taormina, J. (1987). Detection of the traversability of surfaces by crawling and walking infants. *Journal of Experimental Psychology: Human Perception and Performance,* **13**(4), 533–544.

Gibson, E. J., & Schmuckler, M. A. (1989). Going somewhere: An ecological and experimental approach to development of mobility. *Ecological Psychology,* **1**(1), 3–25.

Gibson, E. J., & Walk, R. D. (1960). The "visual cliff." *Scientific American,* **202,** 64–71.

Gibson, E. J., & Walker, A. S. (1984). Development of knowledge of visual-tactile affordances of substance. *Child Development,* **55,** 453–460.

Gibson, J. J. (1962). Observations on active touch. *Psychological Review,* **69**(6), 477–491.

Gibson, J. J. (1966). *The senses considered as perceptual systems.* Boston: Houghton Mifflin.

Gibson, J. J. (1979). *The ecological approach to visual perception.* Boston: Houghton Mifflin.

Gibson, J. J., & Gibson, E. J. (1955). Perceptual learning: Differentiation or enrichment? *Psychological Review,* **62,** 32–41.

Goldfield, E. C. (1989). Transition from rocking to crawling: Postural constraints in infant movement. *Developmental Psychology,* **25,** 913–919.

Goldfield, E. C. (1993). Dynamic systems in development: Action systems. In L. B. Smith & E. Thelen (Eds.), *A dynamic systems approach to development: Applications.* Cambridge, MA: MIT Press.

Grieve, D. W., & Gear, R. J. (1966). The relationships between length of stride, step frequency, time of swing and speed of walking for children and adults. *Ergonomics,* **5**(9), 379–399.

Gustafson, G. E. (1984). Effects of the ability to locomote on infants' social and exploratory behaviors: An experimental study. *Developmental Psychology,* **20**(3), 397–405.

Harlow, H. F., & Mears, C. E. (1978). The nature of complex, unlearned responses. In M. Lewis & L. A. Rosenblum (Eds.), *The development of affect.* New York: Plenum.

Hein, A., & Diamond, R. M. (1972). Locomotor space as a prerequisite for acquiring visually guided reaching in kittens. *Journal of Comparative and Physiological Psychology,* **81**(3), 394–398.

Heinrichs, M., Bigbee, M., & Pick, H. L. (1991, April). *The margin of safety in moving past a barrier.* Poster presented at the meeting of the Society for Research in Child Development, Seattle.

Held, R., & Hein, A. (1963). Movement-produced stimulation in the development of visually guided behavior. *Journal of Comparative and Physiological Psychology,* **56**(5), 872–876.

134

Hirschfeld, H., & Forssberg, H. (1994). Epigenetic development of postural responses for sitting during infancy. *Experimental Brain Research,* **97,** 528–540.

Hofsten, C. Von, & Fazel-Zandy, S. (1984). Development of visually guided hand orientation in reaching. *Journal of Experimental Child Psychology,* **38,** 208–219.

Hudson, R. R., & Johnson, W. (1976). Elementary rock climbing mechanics. *International Journal of Mechanical Engineering Education,* **4**(4), 357–367.

Ingle, D., & Cooke, J. (1977). The effects of viewing distance upon size preference of frogs for prey. *Vision Research,* **17,** 1009–1019.

Kermoian, R., & Campos, J. J. (1988). Locomotor experience: A facilitator of spatial cognitive development. *Child Development,* **59,** 908–917.

Kinsella-Shaw, J. M., Shaw, B., & Turvey, M. T. (1992). Perceiving "walk-on-able" slopes. *Ecological Psychology,* **4**(4), 223–239.

Klatzky, R. L., Lederman, S. J., & Matula, D. E. (1993). Haptic exploration in the presence of vision. *Journal of Experimental Psychology: Human Perception and Performance,* **19,** 726–743.

Klatzky, R. L., Lederman, S. J., & Reed, C. (1987). There's more to touch than meets the eye: The salience of object attributes for haptics with and without vision. *Journal of Experimental Psychology: General,* **116,** 356–369.

Klatzky, R. L., Lederman, S. J., & Reed, C. (1989). Haptic integration of object properties: Texture, hardness, and planar contour. *Journal of Experimental Psychology: Human Perception and Performance,* **15,** 45–57.

Kohler, W. (1925). *The mentality of apes* (E. Winter, Trans.). New York: Harcourt, Brace & World.

Konner, M. (1976). Maternal care, infant behavior and development among the Kalahari Desert San. In R. B. Lee & I. DeVore (Eds.), *Kalahari hunter-gatherers.* Cambridge, MA: Harvard University Press.

Koslowski, B., & Bruner, J. S. (1972). Learning to use a lever. *Child Development,* **43,** 790–799.

Lashley, K. S. (1960). *The neuropsychology of Lashley: Selected papers.* New York: McGraw-Hill.

Lederman, S. J., & Klatzky, R. L. (1987). Hand movements: A window into haptic object recognition. *Cognitive Psychology,* **19,** 342–368.

Lederman, S. J., & Klatzky, R. L. (1993). Extracting object properties through haptic exploration. *Acta Psychologica,* **84,** 29–40.

Lee, D. N. (1974). Visual information during locomotion. In R. B. MacLeod & H. L. Pick (Eds.), *Perception: Essays in honor of James J. Gibson.* Ithaca, NY: Cornell University Press.

Lee, D. N. (1980). The optic flow field: The foundation of vision. *Philosophical Transactions of the Royal Society of London,* **290,** 169–179.

Lee, D. N. (1994). Body-environment coupling. In U. Neisser (Ed.), *The perceived self: Ecological and interpersonal sources of self-knowledge.* Cambridge: Cambridge University Press.

Lee, D. N., & Aronson, E. (1974). Visual proprioceptive control of standing in human infants. *Perception and Psychophysics,* **15,** 529–532.

Lee, D. N., & Lishman, J. R. (1975). Visual proprioceptive control of stance. *Journal of Human Movement Studies,* **1,** 87–95.

Lee, D. N., & Reddish, P. E. (1981). Plummeting gannets: A paradigm of ecological optics. *Nature,* **293,** 293–294.

Lee, D. N., & Thompson, J. A. (1982). Vision in action: The control of locomotion. In D. Ingle (Ed.), *Analysis of visual behavior.* Cambridge, MA: MIT Press.

Leeuwen, L. van, Smitsman, A., & Leeuwen, C. van. (1994). Affordances, perceptual complexity, and the development of tool use. *Journal of Experimental Psychology: Human Perception and Performance,* **20,** 174–191.

Lishman, J. R., & Lee, D. N. (1973). The autonomy of visual kinaesthesis. *Perception, 2,* 287–294.

Lockman, J. J. (1984). The development of detour ability during infancy. *Child Development, 55,* 482–491.

Lockman, J. J., Ashmead, D. H., & Bushnell, E. W. (1984). The development of anticipatory hand orientation during infancy. *Journal of Experimental Child Psychology, 37,* 176–186.

MacKay, D. G. (1982). The problems of flexibility, fluency, and speed-accuracy trade-off in skilled behavior. *Psychological Review, 89,* 483–506.

Mahler, M., Pine, F., & Bergman, A. (1975). *The psychological birth of the human infant.* New York: Basic.

Mark, L. S. (1987). Eyeheight-scaled information about affordances: A study of sitting and stair climbing. *Journal of Experimental Psychology: Human Perception and Performance, 13*(3), 361–370.

Mark, L. S., Baillet, J. A., Craver, K. D., Douglas, S. D., & Fox, T. (1990). What an actor must do in order to perceive the affordance for sitting. *Ecological Psychology, 2*(4), 325–366.

Mark, L. S., & Vogele, D. (1987). A biodynamic basis for perceived categories of action: A study of sitting and stair climbing. *Journal of Motor Behavior, 19*(3), 367–384.

Martinsen, H. (1982). A naturalistic study of young children's explorations away from the caregiver. *International Journal of Behavioral Development, 5,* 217–228.

McCaskill, C. L., & Wellman, B. L. (1938). A study of common motor achievements at the preschool ages. *Child Development, 9,* 141–150.

McCollum, G., & Leen, T. K. (1989). Form and exploration of mechanical stability limits in erect stance. *Journal of Motor Behavior, 21,* 225–244.

McGraw, M. (1935). *Growth: A study of Johnny and Jimmy.* New York: Appleton-Century.

McGraw, M. B. (1940). Neuromuscular development of the human infant as exemplified in the achievement of erect locomotion. *Journal of Pediatrics, 17,* 747–771.

McGraw, M. B. (1945). *The neuromuscular maturation of the human infant.* New York: Columbia University Press.

McGraw, M. B. (1946). Maturation of behavior. In L. Carmichael (Ed.), *Manual of child psychology* (1st ed.). New York: Wiley.

Meltzoff, A. N., & Borton, R. W. (1979). Intermodal matching by human neonates. *Nature, 282,* 403–404.

Nashner, L. M. (1977). Fixed patterns of rapid postural responses among leg muscles during stance. *Experimental Brain Research, 30,* 13–24.

Nashner, L. M., & McCollum, G. (1985). The organization of human postural movements: A formal basis and experimental synthesis. *Behavioral and Brain Sciences, 8,* 135–172.

Nelson, R. C., & Osterhoudt, R. G. (1971). Effects of altered slope and speed on the biomechanics of running. *Medicine and Sport, 6,* 220–224.

Palmer, C. E. (1944). Studies of the center of gravity of the human body. *Child Development, 15,* 99–163.

Palmer, C. F. (1987, April). *Between a rock and a hard place: Babies in tight spaces.* Poster presented at the meeting of the Society for Research in Child Development, Baltimore.

Palmer, C. F. (1989a). The discriminating nature of infants' exploratory actions. *Developmental Psychology, 25,* 885–893.

Palmer, C. F. (1989b, April). *Max Headroom: Toddlers locomoting through doorways.* Paper presented at the meeting of the Society for Research in Child Development, Kansas City, MO.

Piaget, J. (1952). *The origins of intelligence in children.* New York: International Universities Press.

Piaget, J. (1954). *The construction of reality in the child.* New York: Free Press.

Piaget, J. (1961). *The mechanisms of perception* (G. N. Seagrim, Trans.). New York: Basic.

Pick, H. L. (1989). Motor development: The control of action. *Developmental Psychology*, **25**, 867–870.

Proffitt, D. R., Bhalla, M., Gossweiler, R., & Midgett, J. (1995). Perceiving geographical slant. *Psychonomic Bulletin and Review*, **2**, 409–428.

Pufall, P. B., & Dunbar, C. (1992). Perceiving whether or not the world affords stepping onto and over: A developmental study. *Ecological Psychology*, **4**(1), 17–38.

Rader, N., Bausano, M., & Richards, J. E. (1980). On the nature of the visual-cliff-avoidance response in human infants. *Child Development*, **51**, 61–68.

Richards, J. E., & Rader, N. (1981). Crawling-onset age predicts visual cliff avoidance in infants. *Journal of Experimental Psychology: Human Perception and Performance*, **7**(2), 382–387.

Richards, J. E., & Rader, N. (1983). Affective, behavioral, and avoidance responses on the visual cliff: Effects of crawling onset age, crawling experience, and testing age. *Psychophysiology*, **20**(6), 633–642.

Rieser, J. J., Doxsey, P. A., McCarrell, N. S., & Brooks, P. H. (1982). Wayfinding and toddlers' use of information from an aerial view of a maze. *Developmental Psychology*, **18**, 714–720.

Rieser, J. J., Pick, H. L., Ashmead, D. H., & Garing, A. E. (1995). Calibration of human locomotion and models of perceptual-motor organization. *Journal of Experimental Psychology: Human Perception and Performance*, **21**, 480–497.

Rochat, P. (1987). Mouthing and grasping in neonates: Evidence for early detection of what hard or soft substances afford for action. *Infant Behavior and Development*, **10**, 435–449.

Rochat, P. (1989). Object manipulation and exploration in 2–5-month-old infants. *Developmental Psychology*, **25**, 871–884.

Rovee-Collier, C., Greco-Vigorito, C., & Hayne, H. (1993). The time-window hypothesis: Implications for categorization and memory modification. *Infant Behavior and Development*, **16**, 149–176.

Ruff, H. A. (1984). Infants' manipulative exploration of objects: Effects of age and object characteristics. *Developmental Psychology*, **20**, 9–20.

Sanderson, P. M., McNeese, M. D., & Zaff, B. S. (1994). Handling complex real-world data with two cognitive engineering tools: COGENT and MacSHAPA. *Behavior Research Methods, Instruments, and Computers*, **26**, 117–124.

Sanderson, P. M., Scott, J. J. P., Johnston, T., Mainzer, J., Watanabe, L. M., & James, J. M. (1994). MacSHAPA and the enterprise of Exploratory Sequential Data Analysis (ESDA). *International Journal of Human-Computer Studies*, **41**(5), 633–681.

Scarr, S., & Salapatek, P. (1970). Patterns of fear development during infancy. *Merrill-Palmer Quarterly*, **16**, 53–90.

Schiff, W. (1965). Perception of impending collision: A study of visually directed avoidant behavior. *Psychological Monographs: General and Applied*, **79**(11, Serial No. 604).

Schmuckler, M. A. (1996). Development of visually guided locomotion: Barrier crossing by toddlers. *Ecological Psychology*, **8**, 209–236.

Schmuckler, M. A., & Gibson, E. J. (1989). The effect of imposed optical flow on guided locomotion in young walkers. *British Journal of Developmental Psychology*, **7**, 193–206.

Shirley, M. M. (1931). *The first two years: A study of 25 babies: Vol. 1. Postural and locomotor development.* Minneapolis: University of Minnesota Press.

Shumway-Cook, A., & Woollacott, M. H. (1985). The growth of stability: Postural control from a developmental perspective. *Journal of Motor Behavior*, **17**, 131–147.

Siegler, R. S., & Jenkins, E. (1989). *How children discover new strategies.* Hillsdale, NJ: Erlbaum.

Slater, A., & Morison, V. (1985). Shape constancy and slant perception at birth. *Perception*, **14**, 337–344.

Slater, A., Morison, V., & Somers, M. (1988). Orientation discrimination and cortical function in the human newborn. *Perception*, **17**, 597–602.

Smith, L. B., & Thelen, E. (1993). *A dynamic systems approach to development: Applications.* Cambridge, MA: MIT Press.

Stoffregen, T. A. (1985). Flow structure versus retinal location in the optical control of stance. *Journal of Experimental Psychology: Human Perception and Performance, 11,* 554–565.

Stoffregen, T., Adolph, K. E., Thelen, E., Gorday, K. M., & Sheng, Y. Y. (in press). Toddlers' postural adaptations to different support surfaces. *Motor Control.*

Stoffregen, T. A., & Riccio, G. E. (1988). An ecological theory of orientation and the vestibular system. *Psychological Review, 95,* 3–14.

Stoffregen, T. A., Schmuckler, M. A., & Gibson, E. J. (1987). Use of central and peripheral optical flow in stance and locomotion in young walkers. *Perception, 16,* 113–119.

Super, C. (1976). Environmental effects on motor development: The case of African infant precocity. *Developmental Medicine and Child Neurology, 8,* 561–567.

Sutherland, D. H., Olshen, R., Cooper, L., & Woo, S. (1980). The development of mature gait. *Journal of Bone and Joint Surgery, 62A,* 336–353.

Thelen, E. (1984). Learning to walk: Ecological demands and phylogenetic constraints. *Advances in Infancy Research, 3,* 213–260.

Thelen, E. (1986). Treadmill-elicited stepping in seven-month-old infants. *Child Development, 57,* 1498–1506.

Thelen, E. (1989). The (re)discovery of motor development: Learning new things from an old field. *Developmental Psychology, 25,* 946–949.

Thelen, E. (1995). Motor development: A new synthesis. *American Psychologist, 50,* 79–95.

Thelen, E., & Adolph, K. E. (1992). Arnold L. Gesell: The paradox of nature and nurture. *Developmental Psychology, 28,* 368–380.

Thelen, E., & Fisher, D. M. (1982). Newborn stepping: An explanation for a "disappearing reflex." *Developmental Psychology, 18,* 760–775.

Thelen, E., Fisher, D. M., & Ridley-Johnson, R. (1984). The relationship between physical growth and a newborn reflex. *Infant Behavior and Development, 7,* 479–493.

Thelen, E., & Smith, L. B. (1994). *A dynamic systems approach to the development of cognition and action.* Cambridge, MA: MIT Press.

Thelen, E., & Ulrich, B. D. (1991). Hidden skills: A dynamic systems analysis of treadmill stepping during the first year. *Monographs of the Society for Research in Child Development, 56*(1, Serial No. 223).

Titzer, R. (1995, March). *The developmental dynamics of understanding transparency.* Paper presented at the meeting of the Society for Research in Child Development, Indianapolis.

Ulrich, B., Thelen, E., & Niles, D. (1990). Perceptual determinants of action: Stair-climbing choices of infants and toddlers. In J. E. Clark, & J. Humphrey (Eds.), *Advances in motor development research* (Vol. 3). New York: AMS.

Vereijken, B., Adolph, K. E., Denny, M. A., Fadl, Y., Gill, S. V., & Lucero, A. A. (1995). Development of infant crawling: Balance constraints on interlimb coordination. In G. Bardy, R. J. Bootsma, & Y. Guiard (Eds.), *Studies in perception and action III.* Hillsdale, NJ: Erlbaum.

Vereijken, B., van Emmerick, R. E. A., Whiting, H. T. A., & Newell, K. M. (1993). Free(z)ing degrees of freedom in skill acquisition. *Journal of Motor Behavior, 24,* 133–142.

Walk, R. D. (1966). The development of depth perception in animals and human infants. *Monographs of the Society for Research in Child Development, 31*(5, Serial No. 107), 82–108.

Walk, R. D., & Gibson, E. J. (1961). A comparative and analytical study of visual depth perception. *Psychological Monographs, 75*(15, Whole No. 519).

Walker, J. (1989). The mechanics of rock climbing; or, Surviving the ultimate physics exam. *Scientific American, 260,* 118–121.

Warren, W. H. (1984). Perceiving affordances: Visual guidance of stair climbing. *Journal of Experimental Psychology: Human Perception and Performance, 10*(5), 683–703.

Warren, W. H., Blackwell, A. W., Kurtz, K. J., Hatsopoulos, N. G., & Kalish, M. L. (1991). On the sufficiency of the velocity field for perception of heading. *Biological Cybernetics,* **65,** 311–320.

Warren, W. H., Mestre, D. R., Blackwell, A. W., & Morris, M. W. (1991). Perception of circular heading from optical flow. *Journal of Experimental Psychology: Human Perception and Performance,* **17,** 28–43.

Warren, W. H., Morris, M. W., & Kalish, M. (1988). Perception of translational heading from optical flow. *Journal of Experimental Psychology: Human Perception and Performance,* **14,** 646–660.

Warren, W. H., & Whang, S. (1987). Visual guidance of walking through apertures: Body-scaled information for affordances. *Journal of Experimental Psychology: Human Perception and Performance,* **13,** 371–383.

Wechsler, M. A. (1995). *Strategy acquisition and strategy choice in infants descending slopes.* Unpublished senior honors thesis, Middlebury College, Middlebury, VT.

Wechsler, M. A., & Adolph, K. E. (1995, April). *Learning new ways of moving: Variability in infants' discovery and selection of motor strategies.* Poster presented at the meeting of the Society for Research in Child Development, Indianapolis.

Willatts, P. (1989). Development of problem-solving in infancy. In A. Slater & G. Bremner (Eds.), *Infant development.* Hillsdale, NJ: Erlbaum.

Woollacott, M. H. (1986). Postural control and development. In M. G. Wade & H. T. A. Whiting (Eds.), *Themes in motor development.* Dordrecht: Martinus Nijhoff.

Woollacott, M., Debu, M., & Mowatt, M. (1987). Neuromuscular control of posture in the infant and child: Is vision dominant? *Journal of Motor Behavior,* **19,** 167–186.

Woollacott, M. H., Hofsten, C. Von, & Rosblad, B. (1988). Relation between muscle response onset and body segmental movements during postural perturbations in humans. *Experimental Brain Research,* **72,** 593–604.

Woollacott, M. H., & Jensen, J. L. (1992). Posture and locomotion. In H. Heuer & S. Keele (Eds.), *Handbook of perception and action: Vol. 2. Motor skills.* London: Academic.

Woollacott, M. H., & Shumway-Cook, A. (1990). Changes in postural control across the life span—a systems approach. *Physical Therapy,* **70,** 799–807.

Woollacott, M. H., & Sveistrup, H. (1992). Changes in the sequencing and timing of muscle response coordination associated with developmental transitions in balance abilities. *Human Movement Science,* **11,** 23–36.

Yonas, A. (1981). Infants' response to optical information for collision. In R. Aslin, J. Alberts, & M. Peterson (Eds.), *Development of perception: Vol. 2. The visual system.* New York: Academic.

Zelazo, P. R. (1982). The year-old infant: A period of major cognitive change. In T. G. Bever (Ed.), *Regression in mental development: Basic phenomena and theories.* Hillsdale, NJ: Erlbaum.

ACKNOWLEDGMENTS

I gratefully acknowledge the support of Esther Thelen, the members of the Indiana University Infant Motor Development Laboratory, and the 29 families who participated in this study. John Waltke designed the sloping walkway, and Dexter Gormley maintained equipment. Marion Eppler, Eleanor Gibson, Ulric Neisser, Cynthia O'Dell, and Esther Thelen guided the design of the study. Many students at Indiana University, Carnegie Mellon University, and Middlebury College assisted with data collection, coding, and analyses, especially Tina Baldwin, Kevin Byrne, Mark Denny, Carolina Diaz-Peroza, Shannon Pursifull, and Melissa Wechsler-Clearfield. Anthony Avolio and Barbara Thompson assisted in all stages of data coding and analyses and helped with the preparation of the manuscript, figures, and tables. Martha Alibali, Anthony Avolio, Bennett Bertenthal, Eleanor Gibson, Roberta Klatzky, Robert Siegler, Esther Thelen, Barbara Thompson, and two anonymous reviewers provided many suggestions for improving the manuscript.

This work was supported by National Institute of Child Health and Human Development (NICHHD) grants MH10226-02 and HD33486-02, a Sigma Xi grant-in-aid-of-research award, and a faculty development grant from Carnegie Mellon University to Karen Adolph. Additional support for data collection was provided by NICHHD grant HD22830 to Esther Thelen and by funding from the Emory Cognition Project to Ulric Neisser. Portions of this research were part of Karen Adolph's doctoral thesis. Portions were also presented at the meetings of the Society for Research in Child Development in New Orleans in April 1993 and in Indianapolis in March 1995.

Address correspondence concerning this *Monograph* to Karen E. Adolph at the Department of Psychology, New York University, 6 Washington Place, Room 401, New York, NY 10003, or adolph@psych.nyu.edu.

COMMENTARY

NEW PARADIGMS AND NEW ISSUES:
A COMMENT ON EMERGING THEMES
IN THE STUDY OF MOTOR DEVELOPMENT

Bennett I. Bertenthal and Steven M. Boker

It is widely acknowledged that the field of motor development is going through a renaissance in which new theories and methods are emerging that can be generalized to a much broader cross section of developmental psychology (Bertenthal & Clifton, in press). The longitudinal study described in this *Monograph* adds further credence to this claim. It is an excellent example of why research on motor development now extends well beyond traditional questions and concerns.

During the first half of this century, the study of motor development was oriented primarily toward descriptive changes in behavior that were viewed as almost a direct readout of the maturation of the central nervous system. Although this orientation resulted in detailed observations that offered a wealth of information about sequential changes in motor performance, the theoretical thrust stymied research into the process of development. Once it was acknowledged that motor performance depends intimately on its perceptual modulation (Bernstein, 1967; Gibson, 1979), the emphasis gradually shifted from merely describing motor development to understanding how behaviors are initially organized and fine-tuned with perceptual experience and practice.

Following in this new tradition, the current *Monograph* is concerned with developmental changes in the control and modulation of one of the most

The writing of this Commentary was supported by National Institutes of Health grant HD16196 and National Science Foundation grant SBE-9704764. Correspondence concerning this Commentary should be directed to Bennett I. Bertenthal, Department of Psychology, Gilmer Hall, University of Virginia, Charlottesville VA 22903-2477.

important skills available to all humans—locomotion. The author, Karen Adolph, focuses on how selection and control of different modes of locomotion become increasingly adapted to local surface conditions as a function of age and experience. From a design standpoint, this study is a tour de force employing a longitudinal paradigm and multiple measures addressing how locomotor performance changes as a function of age, home and laboratory experience, and body composition and how it changes as children progress from crawling to walking. We are indebted to Adolph for this *Monograph* because it provides not only an extremely rich data set but also provocative and compelling interpretations of how children learn to modulate their locomotor responses during early development.

Although we withhold final judgment about some specific interpretations and conclusions, our tactic is not to dwell on these points of possible contention but rather to highlight some general themes. In particular, we discuss how the current *Monograph* is relevant to four specific themes that are foundational to contemporary research on the development of perception and action: (1) reciprocity between perception and action, (2) prospective control of behavior, (3) variation and selection in the development of new behaviors, and (4) contributions of age and experience.

Reciprocity between Perception and Action

All successful actions, such as visual tracking, reaching, and locomotion, are coupled to the spatial layout (Bertenthal, 1996). As such, these actions demand that motor responses be scaled to the local situation and that they change in response to variations in these conditions. In most situations, local conditions change not only in response to variations in spatial layout but also as a function of performing the action. Consider, for example, an adult traversing a path that begins sloping downward. As this individual begins walking down the hill, the perceived slant changes continuously, as do the necessary muscle torques that are produced to negotiate the hill successfully. It is for this reason that we claim that perception and action are mutual and reciprocal. Successful performance depends on differentiating and selecting the necessary perceptual information and matching that information to the coordination and control of the appropriate motor synergies.

When adults encounter a novel or unfamiliar situation, such as a very steep hill, it is likely that they engage in some perceptual exploration before proceeding. The goal of this exploration is not to determine the specific incline of the hill but rather to determine whether they possess the necessary strength and balance to walk or slide down the hill or whether they should perhaps avoid the hill altogether. It is thus essential for them to explore not only the perceptual characteristics of the sloping surface but also the relation between the slope and their own biomechanical properties. The dual demands of this task require that perceptual exploration be multimodal and involve both the self and the spatial layout.

In this *Monograph,* multimodal exploration and differentiation of perceptual information are considered essential to successful performance descending the slopes. Evidence is presented to suggest that infants visually and haptically explore the sloping surfaces and that they also shift positions to explore different locomotor methods before descending. Collectively, these data suggest that infants learn through experience to match the surface properties of the slopes with their own biomechanical properties and then select a locomotor strategy contingent on this information. Of course, this conclusion is not a logical necessity given the design of the study, but it is bolstered by the finding that few infants transferred their slope boundaries when shifting from crawling to walking. What, then, are the implications of this research?

From a logical perspective, improved performance descending slopes could be a function of improved perceptual differentiation of the slopes, improved strength and balance while locomoting, or specifically scaling the perceptual information to the motor responses. If learning to differentiate slopes perceptually was the rate-limiting factor, then locomotor status (crawling vs. walking) should not have influenced performance descending slopes. If, however, differences in strength and balance or differences in the coordination of perception and action are responsible for performance, then locomotor status should influence performance. Interestingly, a majority of infants showed a decline in performance descending slopes following the transition to walking. It is thus clear that perception of the slope per se is not sufficient to explain performance, but the status of biomechanical capacity versus perceptuomotor coordination for explaining developmental changes in performance remains something of an open question.

At the risk of introducing additional complexities into this discussion, we submit that precise differentiation between biomechanical status and perceptuomotor coordination may not in fact be possible. Although biomechanical capacities depend partially on the activation of muscles, these capacities depend also on balancing passive forces (intersegmental forces, gravity, etc.) with the active forces produced by muscles (Zernicke & Schneider, 1993). As such, biomechanical status depends as much on the perception of additional internal and external forces as it does on the production of muscular forces. Thus, biomechanical status cannot be truly distinguished from perceptuomotor coordination. It is primarily for this reason that perceptual modulation in conjunction with the scaling of response synergies plays such a dominant role in the development of locomotion as well as every other fundamental motor skill.

Prospective Control of Behavior

It is essential that we learn to control future actions in order to ensure smooth and safe movements (Bertenthal, 1996; von Hofsten, 1993). The inertia of the limbs and the time lags inherent in neural conduction demand some anticipation of future actions. If anticipation were not possible, actions would become staccatic and sometimes unsafe. Consider, for example, reaching for an object while leaning to the side. If the performer does not anticipate how reaching will offset his or her balance, it is quite possible that the necessary compensation for the change in posture will occur too late and that the person will topple over.

During early infancy, there are some remarkable examples of prospective behavior over short time scales. For example, Haith (1994) reported that 2- and 3-month-old infants begin to show anticipatory fixations to the appearance of a target that alternates over time between the left and the right sides of a screen. Also, von Hofsten (1980, 1983) showed how infants could reach for moving objects and intercept them at various speeds up to 120 centimeters per second. The evidence from von Hofsten's studies revealed that, when attempting to intercept an object, infants timed their reaches by aiming their hand to a future location. Similar findings are reported in more recent studies (Bertenthal & von Hofsten, in press; Robin, Berthier, & Clifton, 1996). Most of these examples represent anticipation over very brief durations lasting 1 second or less. By contrast, prospective control of locomotion includes longer time scales and multiple sources of perceptual information.

Consider next the type of prospective control necessary for traversing a surface of support. Most surfaces available for locomotion vary along many dimensions, including slant, rigidity, smoothness, presence of obstacles, discontinuities in the path, and so on. Typically, these properties are specified in advance by spatiotemporal changes in the optic array so that observers have sufficient time to adapt their locomotor patterns if necessary. Additional information is available through haptic exploration and by testing different postures on the support surface, but these sources of proximal information require some interruption of locomotion for perceptual exploration to proceed. Thus, prospective control of locomotion differs markedly if it includes haptic exploration of the surface or further exploration of different locomotor patterns.

Adolph suggests that infants perceptually explore the slopes before selecting a response and descending. Regrettably, it is somewhat difficult to confirm this interpretation because visual exploration is not measured directly but only inferred from the latency to begin descending. In spite of this reservation, it is clear that latency to select a locomotor strategy and proceed down the slope continues to decrease with experience. As such, the evidence suggests (although it does not confirm) that visual exploration decreases with experience.

By contrast, haptic exploration shows a more complex developmental pattern. The data suggest that haptic forms of exploration are initially frequent, but decrease with crawling experience, and then increase again with walking experience. In view of this pattern of findings, it is not entirely clear how to interpret the process by which infants select a locomotor strategy before proceeding down a slope. We concur with Adolph that perceptual information guides the response, but we find it difficult to ascertain how much of the measured exploratory activity is directed specifically toward acquiring information to control the response. Indeed, it is difficult to determine whether any of the haptic information was really required, especially since the relevant exploratory behaviors were not observed on every trial. Conceivably, these behaviors could represent nonspecific responses that are independent of the task, or they could represent some opportunity to explore the surface prior to selecting a locomotor strategy for descending the slope.

Even if the latter interpretation is correct, we want to emphasize that, while haptic exploration offers additional information for selecting a locomotor strategy, it certainly does not offer the same type of distal prospective control available from visual information. It thus appears that perceptual information is used for multiple functions in the selection and guidance of locomotion. An important goal for future research is to clarify how different sources of perceptual information are complementary and contribute in different ways to performance.

Variation and Selection

Traditional views of development focus on sequential patterns of change with little attention directed toward variability in performance. As a consequence, development is often conceptualized as periods of stable performance interrupted by brief periods of variability and abrupt changes in behavior. Siegler (1995) depicts this view of development as a staircase and contrasts it with a radically different view depicted as a series of overlapping waves or functions. The advantage of the latter view is that it acknowledges the availability of multiple responses as part of the behavioral repertoire; these responses are elicited with different probabilities as a function of task, developmental status, and intrinsic goals of the child. When viewed from this perspective, variability in performance is no longer simply a reflection of measurement error or other sources of error variance but rather a meaningful source of information about the behavior of the child.

Although this view of variation in performance has not yet received much empirical attention, there is already some evidence suggesting that variation can be associated with flexibility or adaptability rather than with error or inconsistent results. Consider, for example, the findings from a classic study investigating the pistol-shooting performance of a group of novices and experts (Arutyunyan, Gurfinkel, & Mirsky, 1969). As expected, the likelihood of hitting the center of the target was more varible for novice pistol shooters than for expert shooters, but measures of limb movements revealed more variability by the experts than by the novices. Specifically, novices tended to freeze degrees of freedom and point their pistols stiffly at the target, whereas experts tended to aim their pistols by continuously moving their wrists relative to their shoulders to compensate for slight changes in internal and external conditions. This continuous shifting or movement of the arm is often viewed as variability in performance, but this form of variability represents exactly the type of flexibility necessary to optimize performance.

In the *Monograph*, considerable attention was devoted to interindividual as well as intraindividual variability. One of the most striking findings to emerge is that infants show considerable variation in their selection of locomotor strategies. It is especially noteworthy that infants show variation within sessions, but this variation is far from random. On uphill slopes, infants rarely showed variation in strategies, but they did on downhill slopes, especially those that exceeded the slope boundaries. Adolph offers some provocative hypotheses as to how and why this variation emerges. Most important, she rejects the notion that these new strategies emerge through explicit instruction or prescription. Instead, she offers the intriguing possibility that learning follows a stochastic process in which neurophysiological, biomechanical, and task constraints conspire together to induce new movement patterns. For example, the steepness of some slopes coupled with the stiffness of the arms may be sufficient to turn infants around when they begin to crawl down these slopes. Once these behaviors are introduced by chance, infants will tend to store and repeat those that are successful.

Similar interpretations have been advanced recently to explain the transition from belly crawling to hands-and-knees crawling (Adolph, Vereijken, & Denny, in press; Freedland & Bertenthal, 1994) and to explain improvements in the straightness and accuracy of reaching (Berthier, 1996). These interpretations share a perspective with recent neural models of development that propose that stochastic outcomes will be based on the complementary processes of cooperation and competition (Edelman, 1992; Kaas, 1991). Neural patterns stimulated by high levels of activation will tend to dominate patterns stimulated by lower levels of activation. Repeated experiences with these activation patterns will lead to structural changes in the brain. By analogy, neural net models offer a method for explaining behavioral development as well, but many important questions remain. In particular, it is difficult to determine why some actions are valued and repeated while others are not. Clearly, the valuation of an action depends on whether it is successful, which could easily change as a function of development as well as the situation.

In the case of descending a slope, a successful response no doubt depends on the motor competence of the child, the steepness of the slope, the willingness to take risks, etc. This is clearly a multivariate problem, but it is not clear whether all these variables contribute to the locomotor response selected by the child. Although it is reasonable to postulate that many simple motor skills develop specifically as means of minimizing energy (Bertenthal & Clifton, in press), there is a hierarchy of goals associated with the slope task, and minimization of energy is probably competing with a number of other goals, such as avoiding danger, increasing novelty, and responding to parents' encouragement. In sum, our understanding of the values or motives driving behavioral performance remains virtually unexplored.

Similarly, our understanding of what infants learn during motor development remains somewhat obscure. Presumably, explicit memory for the specific task is not responsible for improvements in performance because the responses of control infants (tested only three times) did not differ significantly from those of the longitudinal infants. Nevertheless, it seems evident that some form of memory is involved given that performance shows improvements from one testing session to the next. It is quite likely that learning is at least partly a function of adding new locomotor responses to the behavioral repertoire. As infants seek alternatives from a larger number of options, they are more likely to select a successful locomotor response from among those that are available. In essence, then, we contend that infants improve their performance as their response repertoire grows and offers greater flexibility.

Contributions of Age and Experience

Once it is recognized that behaviors develop not in isolation but rather as part of a system of variables that feed back on each other, it becomes a daunting task to begin to identify the developmental correlates of any new skill. In the current *Monograph*, Adolph considers a number of logical candidates, but the results from her analysis of these correlates are not entirely satisfying. Basically, we are left with the conclusion that crawling experience is the best predictor of performance on the slope task. We would like to suggest that a more complete understanding of the complex changes that emerge developmentally requires a multivariate model of development. In the remainder of this section, we expand our discussion to explain why a multivariate model is necessary for analyzing developmental correlates of locomotor performance on slopes and how such a model could offer additional insights into the developmental process.

Locomotor performance was assessed primarily by calculating two depen-

147

dent measures. Slope boundaries represented the steepest slope at which infants would select their standard mode of descent on at least 67% of the trials and fail or refuse (or select alternative locomotor mode) to descend a slope that was 2° greater. Go ratios represented the infant's likelihood of selecting a different locomotor strategy on slopes greater than the slope boundary. This ratio was calculated by dividing the number of trials on which the typical locomotor mode was selected (regardless of whether descent was successful) by the total number of trials. As such, the go ratio is an inverse index of the adaptiveness of infants' responses on unsafe slopes; a higher go ratio indicates that performance is less adaptive. The data for these two measures were analyzed as a function of crawling and walking experience, and the results revealed that slope boundaries increased as a function of experience and that go ratios for unsafe slopes decreased as a function of experience; thus, flexibility and adaptiveness increased with age. It is apparent that important changes in perceptual control of locomotion emerge with development, but the process contributing to these changes requires a more complex model than the one tested in this study.

Adolph correctly considers a large number of theoretically relevant variables that might conceivably contribute to changes in performance with age. These variables include a number of measures of body size (height, weight, head, etc.), crawling proficiency (cycles per second, velocity), and home experience (stairs, furniture, etc.). Bivariate comparisons among these variables and between these variables and go ratios are assessed with data collected at the final crawling session and at the first walking session. Adolph also evaluates whether these experiential variables contribute to locomotor performance above and beyond the contribution of age per se. All these assessments are necessary and valuable in their own right, but insufficient for analyzing the potentially complex multivariate and dynamic process by which these different experiential variables contribute to development.

Many of the predictor variables assessed by Adolph are highly correlated with each other, suggesting that a complete model will need to examine the structure of the covariances between the measured variables. Moreover, it is conceivable that this pattern of covariations changes with age and experience. In order to establish a more complete developmental model of this process, we suggest that all the relevant variables should be analyzed in a structural model. One of many possible models is shown as the path diagram in Figure C1. This particular model hypothesizes three latent constructs: body size, home experience, and crawling proficiency. These latent constructs are then used along with age and crawling experience to predict slope boundaries or go ratios on slopes steeper than the slope boundary. By analyzing all these variables simultaneously, it is possible to observe the independent effects of the predictor variables on locomotor performance (slope boundaries or go ratios), even though the predictor variables are highly intercorrelated.

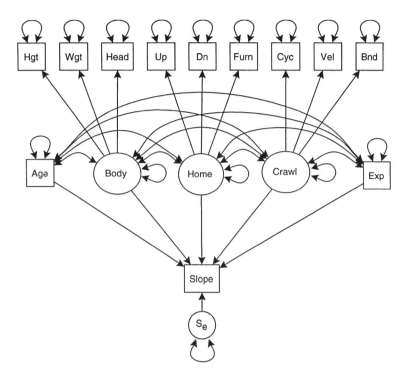

FIGURE C1.—Path diagram of one possible structural equation model designed to estimate the relative independent effects of age, body size, home experience, crawling proficiency, and duration of crawling experience on the measured slope boundary. Hgt = height
of child; wgt = weight of child; head = head circumference; up = ascending stairs; down
= descending stairs; furn = climbing on furniture; cyc = number of crawling or walking
cycles; vel = crawling or walking velocity; bnd = downhill slope boundary.

The advantages of such a model should be immediately evident. First
and foremost, it clarifies and conceptually structures the ways in which the
different predictor and latent variables might be related to the outcome. Second, the creation of such a model allows us to test whether different outcome
variables, such as slope boundaries and go ratios, are functions of the same
or different structural relations. Although the two variables are functionally
related (i.e., go ratios are based on slope boundaries), whether they are measuring the same process is an empirical question. If the pattern of relations
between the predictor and the latent variables differs for the two outcomes,
then it is quite reasonable to conclude that they represent different processes.
Finally, a multigroup extension of this type of structural model allows the
opportunity to test whether the same pattern of relations applies to the perceptual control of crawling and walking. If different variables contribute to
the control of crawling and walking down slopes, then the measured struc-

tural relations between the variables will differ as a function of crawling and walking experience. Regrettably, none of these issues were addressed with the analyses conducted by Adolph. As a consequence, our understanding of the process by which infants learn adaptive control of locomotion on slopes is less complete than it might have been.

One reservation about this multivariate approach concerns the small sample of infants tested longitudinally. In order to compensate for such a small sample, we recommend combining the experimental and control group infants and assessing their performance at the two occasions common to most subjects (the tenth week of crawling and the first week of walking). Complete data from at least 25 infants would then be available for testing different models. Although this strategy cannot ensure that all significant effects will be detected, many of the correlations between predictors and outcomes were very high and may therefore still be detected in a model in which statistical power is marginal.

In the final analysis, we wish to emphasize the importance of developing and fitting such a structural model even if the design of the study lacks sufficient power to test the model statistically. By placing the predictor and latent variables in a specific model that can be visualized and compared to other models, this approach underscores the importance of considering the complex and multivariate relations between the different variables and outcomes. It is for this reason that the task of identifying the different correlates to any developmental process remains a very challenging enterprise (cf. Wohlwill, 1973).

Concluding Comment

In concluding, we commend Adolph for her innovative and creative research. She has pioneered a new paradigm that offers a unique opportunity to observe some of the complex processes involved in the development of locomotion. More generally, her *Monograph* challenges researchers to think about the dynamic and multivariate nature of motor development. Our goal in this Commentary was simply to make this challenge more explicit.

References

Adolph, K. E., Vereijken, B., & Denny, M. A. (in press). Roles of variability and experience in development of crawling. *Child Development*.

Arutyunyan, G., Gurfinkel, V., & Mirsky, M. (1969). Investigation of aiming at a target. *Biophysics*, **13**, 536–538.

Bernstein, N. (1967). *The coordination and regulation of movements*. Oxford: Pergamon.

Bertenthal, B. I. (1996). Origins and early development of perception, action, and representation. *Annual Review of Psychology*, **47**, 431–459.

Bertenthal, B. I., & Clifton, R. (in press). Perception and action. In D. Kuhn & R. Siegler (Eds.), *Handbook of child psychology: Vol. 2. Cognition, perception, and language.* New York: Wiley.

Bertenthal, B. I., & von Hofsten, C. (in press). Development of eye, head, and trunk control as prerequisites for reaching. *Neuroscience and Biobehavioral Reviews.*

Berthier, N. E. (1996). Learning to reach: A mathematical model. *Developmental Psychology,* **32,** 811–823.

Edelman, G. M. (1992). *Bright air, brilliant fire: On the matter of mind.* New York: Basic.

Freedland, R. L., & Bertenthal, B. I. (1994). Developmental changes in interlimb coordination: Transition to hands-and-knees crawling. *Psychological Science,* **5,** 26–32.

Gibson, J. J. (1979). *The ecological approach to visual perception.* Boston: Houghton Mifflin.

Haith, M. M. (1994). Visual expectations as the first step toward the development of future-oriented processes. In M. M. Haith, J. B. Benson, R. J. Roberts, & B. F. Pennington (Eds.), *The development of future-oriented processes.* Chicago: University of Chicago Press.

Kaas, J. H. (1991). Plasticity of sensory and motor maps in adult mammals. *Annual Review of Neuroscience,* **14,** 137–167.

Robin, D. J., Berthier, N. E., & Clifton, R. K. (1996). Infants' predictive reaching for moving objects in the dark. *Developmental Psychology,* **32,** 824–835.

Siegler, R. S. (1995). How does change occur? A microgenetic study of number conservation. *Cognitive Psychology,* **28,** 225–273.

von Hofsten, C. (1980). Predictive reaching for moving objects by human infants. *Journal of Experimental Child Psychology,* **30,** 369–382.

von Hofsten, C. (1983). Catching skills in infancy. *Journal of Experimental Psychology: Human Perception and Performance,* **9,** 75–85.

von Hofsten, C. (1993). Prospective control: A basic aspect of action development. *Human Development,* **36,** 253–270.

Wohlwill, J. (1973). *The study of behavioral development.* New York: Academic.

Zernicke, R. F., & Schneider, K. (1993). Biomechanics and developmental neuromotor control. *Child Development,* **64,** 982–1004.

TOWARD A DEVELOPMENTAL ECOLOGICAL PSYCHOLOGY

Eugene C. Goldfield

Karen Adolph's *Monograph* introduces a new paradigm for studying early adaptive locomotion, how infants match locomotor responses to their local terrain as a function of changes in their own bodies and skills. Adolph was trained in the laboratories of Eleanor Gibson, Esther Thelen, and Ulrich Neisser, and, while this work bears the imprint of these influences, Adolph has clearly found her own voice. Like Eleanor Gibson's pioneering visual cliff studies, Adolph's experiments with infants locomoting in different ways on a sloping walkway provide both a rich naturalistic context and a means for detailed analysis of exploratory and performatory behaviors. The examination of the relation between locomotor skill and the infant's style of approaching inclined surfaces makes this study a prototype for future experiments on the psychophysics of action in the real world as it relates to development, a developmental ecological psychology.

Two landmark longitudinal studies of locomotion provide another source of historical context for this *Monograph:* McGraw's classic observations of the twins Johnny and Jimmy (McGraw, 1945) and the more recent treadmill experiments by Thelen and Ulrich (1991) elucidating the emergence of alternating patterns of stepping. These works represent efforts to understand both the links between individual styles and normative patterns and the potential influences of differential experience during development. Finally, this *Monograph* addresses the difficult question of the relation between perceiving, acting, and knowing, which Neisser discussed in his 1976 *Cognition and Reality.* These three historical threads constitute the organizational framework for my comments on this *Monograph.*

The Requirements of an Ecological Psychology

A distinguishing characteristic of ecological psychology is that it poses questions about the structure of perceptual information based on the functional requirements of different modes of action. The sloping walkway embodies this scientific goal for the study of infant locomotion because it makes possible the measurement of both performatory activity (e.g., style of locomotion) and perceptual exploration as infants navigate through systematically varying inclines. Locomotion is a unique mode of action (Goldfield, 1995; Reed, 1982) and is distinguished from other activities, such as manipulating objects or drinking from a bottle, by the set of nested postures that constitutes its perception-action cycle. Gait transitions in locomotion are apparent during microgenesis, for example, in the coordinative change of a horse's four legs with increases in speed (trot to gallop) as well as during human ontogenesis. Gait transitions are scaled to certain optimality characteristics of the mammalian body, such as metabolic rate (as measured by oxygen consumption) and the threshold of musculoskeletal forces at which bone breaks and tissue tears beyond its elastic limits (see, e.g., Farley & Taylor, 1991).

The achievement of upright stance and walking following a period of crawling is a most notable locomotor transition in human ontogenesis, and this achievement is a focus of Adolph's analysis of the relation between locomotion and the perception of category boundaries for approach or avoidance of certain sloped surfaces. Adolph describes in general terms the postural changes that accompany the transition from crawling to walking, and future work may make it possible to identify the link between specific changes in the organization of functional motor synergies for crawling and walking and changes in their perceptual control. Such a link requires a specification, at least in general terms, of a set of control laws that allow action to be adapted to local conditions.

Control laws seek a description of perceptual information already couched in the language of dynamics, that is, information about the kinematics and kinetics or force requirements of action (Warren, 1988). For example, locomotion is a dissipative system, like a bouncing ball: it dissipates energy and decreases in amplitude unless there is an energy "squirt" at the exact moment in the cycle that will sustain it (Kugler & Turvey, 1987). There is some evidence that infants are able to detect information specifying when in the locomotor cycle to apply a muscular force (a kick) to sustain the cycle. Goldfield, Kay, and Warren (1993) studied how infants explored the timing and force of their own kicking in order to sustain cycles of bouncing while supported upright by a harness attached to a spring. These infants, who had not yet learned to walk, discovered over longitudinal sessions that when they kicked at maximum knee flexion—when the greatest amount of potential energy is stored in the tissues of the legs—they got the highest bounce.

Adolph alludes to this kind of exploration of the information available at the joints during prone rocking, and more work needs to be done to begin to specify how exploration of forces acting on the body may create category boundaries for energy dissipation. A guidepost for pursuing this line of research is Michael Turvey's work on haptic exploration (for a review, see Turvey, 1996).

Among the major findings of Adolph's study is that what was learned about safe and risky slopes during crawling did not transfer to walking. Adolph proposes that these results may be explained by the difference between general purpose and specific exploratory movements. So, for example, rocking while in a crawling position may reveal information useful for learning to balance in order to crawl (see, e.g., Goldfield, 1989), but that information does not seem to transfer to mastering the balance requirements of walking.

Adolph makes a distinction between general and specific information to explain this lack of transfer: while multimodal perceptual exploration ensures that the infant is able to detect general information (e.g., about surfaces) across the range of postural changes encompassing this transition, there is information specific to exploration while in a particular posture. It is also possible to relate "general" and "specific" with respect to the nesting of local perception-action cycles (e.g., movements of the arms) within more global modes of action (the entire body; see, e.g., Reed, 1982). For example, crawling may promote local cycles of exploration related to the proximity of the hands to the support surface, and the boundaries of that local exploratory cycle may be limited by the range of the arm's reach. The upright infant initially uses the arms for balance (e.g., the high guard posture), and this may preclude use of the hands for exploration. Indeed, the crawl pattern may be abandoned because other uses for the hands compete with the support function required of a quadruped (Goldfield, 1995). A more complete theory of the relation between general and specific modes of exploration awaits a further study of the local perception-action cycles embedded within each of the action systems.

Another major finding is that experienced crawlers became overly cautious in going down a slope. Adolph defines the category boundaries for "safe" and "risky" slopes (e.g., the go ratio) on the basis of observations of the infant's approach or avoidance behavior. She proposes that the emergence of caution in the infant's behavior reflects a change from a liberal to a more conservative response criterion: infants begin to match their response to the probability of success. An interpretation based on the direct perception of the affordances of the slope is that the infant's change in behavior depends on some optimality criterion, such as the work required to resist the forces on the slope. The infant's perceptual choices might be organized around the control of forces required to resist falling: steeper slopes may be perceived as requiring greater force than the arms can generate. Indeed, when some infants turn around to go down the slope legs first, they may be capitalizing on the greater strength of the legs to resist the perceived force requirements. An advantage of conceptually linking the gradient of the walkway to forces required to resist falling is that it provides a direct metric between a property of the environment and a capability of the infant (generating certain muscular forces) without recourse to hidden cognitive variables.

Individual Styles and Normative Patterns

Adolph's examination of both individual and group data highlights a recent change in perspective on the development of complex systems, discussed under the more general term *dynamic systems*. A central tenet of this approach is that locomotion is an emergent action system dependent on the confluence of many asynchronously developing elements (Goldfield, 1993; Thelen & Smith, 1994). Because each component of the locomotor system (e.g., neurological changes, muscle strength, skeletal proportions, distribution of mass) has its own rate of development, the particular capability of the system at any point in development may vary widely.

Adolph identifies styles of locomotion with such evocative terms as *Frankenstein gait,* as an indication of a gestalt impression of a collection of kinematic and kinetic variables not measured directly. She also adopts a traditional description of stages to differentiate locomotor achievements. In the spirit of a dynamic systems approach, specification of the asynchronous development of the variables contributing to these styles may be a helpful step in understanding both developmental changes and individual differences in normative (group) patterns.

Dynamic systems approaches, for example, specify how stable patterns of component processes, called *synergies,* emerge from their inherent variability. The appearance of stages of locomotion may reflect the formation and dissolution of locomotor synergies. Synergy formation during locomotor development may involve several tasks, originally proposed by Bernstein in the 1940s and discussed more recently in a volume examining his later work (Latash & Turvey, 1996). The tasks involved in synergy formation (and perhaps in the emergence of locomotor stages) include (1) selecting agonist and antagonist muscles to produce a particular motor trajectory, (2) synchronizing muscles that must contract by different amounts in the same amount of time, and (3) synchronizing limb segments that have different "preferred" frequencies (Turvey & Carello, 1996). The stage of crawling, therefore, may be distinguished by particular limb synchronizations induced by intrinsic asymmetries

155

in the limbs, such as hand preferences (Goldfield, 1989), whereas walking may involve synchronizing the antiphase pattern of stepping with other synergies, including a one-to-one phase locking with respiration (see, e.g., Bramble & Carrier, 1983).

Individual differences in the assembly of synergies that are useful for locomotion may be the result of differences in the achievement of temporal synchronization of the limbs or of the separation of temporal organization from power, for example, regulating muscular forces given certain task demands. Thelen et al. (1993), for example, distinguish individual styles of reaching on the basis of force regulation: some babies flail their arms wildly before achieving a smooth reach, while others hardly move at all, simply looking intently at the target. The former infants need to learn to damp out their enthusiastic limb oscillations, while the latter must learn to scale up their initially quiescent limbs. The regulation of muscular forces may involve the use of perceptual information to set the tunable parameters (e.g, damping and stiffness) of the flexibly assembled dynamic system underlying a particular locomotor pattern.

Decision Making

In explaining why infants approach or avoid a particular walkway, Adolph focuses her attention on the cognitive processes of decision making, as measured, for example, by the go ratio. She proposes that the infant uses a set of exploratory procedures for decision making. These are organized into a framework akin to "test-operate test-exit" (Miller, Galanter, & Pribram, 1986): if a surface looks safe, then proceed; if not, avoid it. This computational model puts all the complexity of the problem of controlling locomotion into internal states and detaches the perception-action cycle from the decision-making process. The task of linking decision-making processes to the perception-action cycle is at the heart of recent work in ecological psychology on the nature of intention.

In his newly translated *On Dexterity and Its Development* (1996), Bernstein distinguishes levels of organization in the system that assembles and tunes skilled movement. At the level of synergy, muscular-articular links become organized into functional groupings. Above this synergy are the levels of space and actions, respectively. At the level of space, the system is able to switch coordination solutions to meet environmental demands, and, at the level of actions, synergies are ordered into sequential structures. The way in which the system orders synergies into sequential organizations (the level of actions) in order to meet the environmental requirements specified at the level of space seems to be precisely what Adolph describes. Infants make moment-to-moment choices in navigating the ground ahead, and they have a number of synergies in their repertoire to make these choices, including taking a quick glance, taking a longer look, probing the surface with their hands and feet while looking at their limbs and at the ground, and exploring alternative locomotor methods. Adolph's work, therefore, provides a foundation for moving the study of infant behavior beyond the level of synergies to the highest levels of organization envisioned by Bernstein and others.

Recent work by Robert Shaw and his colleagues suggests another new direction for understanding infant decision making at Bernstein's level of actions—what these researchers call *intentional dynamics* (Kugler, Shaw, Vincente, & Kinsella-Shaw, 1989–1990; Shaw, Repperger, Kadar, & Sim, 1992). Intentional dynamics links Bernstein's level of synergies and the perception-action cycle with internal decision-making processes by positing a field-like layout of relational variables. From the frame of reference of the environment, these relational variables are called *affordances* (a layout of substances and surfaces that require certain combinations of muscular, gravitational, and Coriolis forces in order to be crawled or walked on). From the frame of reference of action, these relational variables are called *effectivities* (the available action synergies together with tunable parameters that can be used to generate or resist forces). For example, target parameters specify the time, distance, and direction required to contact a target, and manner parameters implement the forces required to move the body to the target over a certain distance and direction. Intending to reach a target establishes a "forward-looking" end point for the perception-action cycle (akin to Neisser's cognitive anticipation) by setting target and manner parameters so that they bring the system from what it is currently doing to the end state.

Adolph's data indicate that inexperienced infants tend to be drawn inexorably toward the goal, rather than stopping at a choice point, and apparently do not notice the available affordances. Intentional dynamics implies that these naive infants may forge ahead because the anticipation of a goal state (the intention to "approach") exerts a greater influence on behavior than perceptual information about available affordances. Conversely, the experienced infant who has explored the available affordances may be overly conservative because the affordance information about slopes is inherently inhibitory; that is, it specifies ways for slowing, stopping, and changing direction. Indeed, much of psychological development from infancy seems to involve the development of inhibitory tendencies on action. The fearful response on the visual cliff is one index of this inhibitory tendency, but it is likely to express itself in more subtle ways as infants get older. The precise nature of the effect of these differentiated inhibitory tendencies on the ever-changing intentions of the developing child awaits further study.

References

Bernstein, N. A. (1996). *On dexterity and its development* (M. L. Latash, Trans.). In M. L. La-tash & M. T. Turvey (Eds.), *Dexterity and its development*. Mahwah, NJ: Erlbaum. (Original work published 1991)

Bramble, D. M., & Carrier, D. R. (1983). Running and breathing in mammals. *Science,* **219,** 251–256.

Farley, C., & Taylor, C. (1991). A mechanical trigger for the trot-gallop transition in horses. *Science,* **253,** 306–308.

Goldfield, E. C. (1989). Transition from rocking to crawling: Postural constraints on infant movement. *Developmental Psychology,* **25,** 913–919.

Goldfield, E. C. (1993). Dynamic systems in development: Action systems. In L. Smith & E. Thelen (Eds.), *Dynamic systems in development: Applications*. Cambridge, MA: MIT Press.

Goldfield, E. C. (1995). *Emergent forms: Origins and early development of human action and percep-tion*. New York: Oxford University Press.

Goldfield, E. C., Kay, B., & Warren, W. H., Jr. (1993). Infant bouncing: The assembly and tuning of an action system. *Child Development,* **64,** 1128–1142.

Kugler, P. N., Shaw, R. E., Vincente, K. J., & Kinsella-Shaw, J. (1989–1990). *Inquiry into inten-tional systems: 1. Issues in ecological physics* (Report No. 30). University of Bielefeld, Re-search Group on Mind and Brain, Perspectives in Theoretical Psychology and the Philos-ophy of Mind.

Kugler, P. N., & Turvey, M. T. (1987). *Information, natural law, and the self-assembly of rhythmic movement*. Hillsdale, NJ: Erlbaum.

Latash, M. L., & Turvey, M. T. (Eds.). (1996). *Dexterity and its development*. Mahwah, NJ: Erl-baum.

McGraw, M. B. (1945). *Neuromuscular maturation of the human infant*. New York: Hafner.

Miller, G., Galanter, E., & Pribram, K. (1986). *Plans and the structure of behavior*. New York: Adams-Bannister-Cox.

Neisser, U. (1976). *Cognition and reality: Principles and implications of cognitive psychology*. San Francisco: Freeman.

Reed, E. S. (1982). An outline of a theory of action systems. *Journal of Motor Behavior,* **14,** 98–134.

Shaw, R. E., Repperger, D. W., Kadar, E., & Sim, M. (1992). The intentional spring: A strategy for modeling systems that learn to perform intentional acts. *Journal of Motor Behavior,* **24,** 3–28.

Thelen, E., Corbetta, D., Kamm, K., Spencer, J. P., Schneider, K., & Zernicke, R. F. (1993). The transition to reaching: Mapping intention and intrinsic dynamics. *Child Development,* **64,** 1058–1098.

Thelen, E., & Smith, L. B. (1994). *A dynamic systems approach to the development of cognition and action*. Cambridge, MA: MIT Press.

Thelen, E., & Ulrich, B. D. (1991). Hidden skills: A dynamic systems analysis of treadmill stepping during the first year. *Monographs of the Society for Research in Child Development,* **56**(1, Serial No. 223).

Turvey, M. T. (1996). Dynamic touch. *American Psychologist,* **51,** 1134–1152.

Turvey, M. T., & Carello, C. (1996). Dynamics of Bernstein's levels of synergies. In M. L. Latash & M. T. Turvey (Eds.), *Dexterity and its development*. Mahwah, NJ: Erlbaum.

Warren, W. H., Jr. (1988). Action modes and laws of control for the visual guidance of action. In O. Meijer & K. Roth (Eds.), *Complex movement behavior: The motor-action controversy*. Amsterdam: Elsevier.

DISCOVERING THE AFFORDANCES OF SURFACES OF SUPPORT

Eleanor J. Gibson

I welcome the opportunity to comment on this *Monograph* since I watched the work progress and consider it a major contribution to our knowledge of behavioral development. I limit my comments to four points, three of them theoretical. The first is very general, perhaps pushing the limits of what is appropriate, but it is a matter of concern to me and possibly to the future of developmental psychology. I begin it with a story, one with a moral, of course.

In an overheard conversation, a remark was made about psychology. A listener, retired from a major psychology department, replied, "Psychology is dead." End of conversation. I have recently feared, myself, that psychology is moribund, that too many of the bright people have given up what should be our territory to neurology, or genetics, or computer science, or philosophy. I feel strongly that psychologists have a legitimate and very important field, that behavior needs to be studied scientifically at its own level, and that regularities (potential laws and progressions) exist that we should be looking for. If we do not undertake this task, the vacuum will be filled by others not properly trained for the job. At Princeton University, for example, there is a new course called "Learning Theory and Epistemology." It is taught by a philosopher (the director of their program on cognitive studies) and an electrical engineer. Where are the psychologists? I am happy to think that the author of this *Monograph* is cultivating our territory.

This *Monograph* reports a substantial and important study of the early development of a universal, basic pattern of human behavior: navigating the world successfully on one's own locomotor power in a layout of surfaces varying in slope. The study is longitudinal, following individual infants before they have any means of locomotion to a point where erect locomotion is

159

safely under the individual's control. Behavioral changes prove to be regular and predictable despite individual differences in timing and minor coping strategies. A longitudinal study is a daunting enterprise (babies get sick, families move away, mothers go to work, etc.), but it has the great potential of uncovering the true course of development. There are surprises here despite the universality of the achievement and despite several classic preexisting studies of locomotor development conducted in the 1930s.

My second comment relates to the theoretical framework that underlies this study. The research fits neatly into the program of what J. J. Gibson called the "ecological approach to perception," which emphasizes two major hypotheses. First, an animal and its environment are reciprocally related. The environment offers supports and constraints that the animal uses if its particular structure and powers permit. Water bugs walk on water, but humans do not. A highly skilled adult performer may be able to walk on a tightrope, but an untrained adult cannot, let alone a child of 12 months. Behavior is mutually determined by these two forces, which vary and interact in complex, dynamic ways. Second, there is also a reciprocal relation between perception and action. What the environment affords for action for any animal must be perceived in order to be acted on. *Affordance* is a unifying concept for this reciprocal relation. It implies that certain possibilities of action exist for any given subject and that the developmental task of the animal (adult human, infant human, or any other creature) is to perceive these possibilities and learn to use them when appropriate opportunities are offered.

Adolph's research has followed a course that illuminates our knowledge of just how this task is accomplished. Environmental situations representing varying affordances are presented to infants over a period of time that allows them to progress to the limits of their physiques and powers in learning how to use (or not try to use) the opportunities the environment offers. We see the babies exploring to obtain appropriate information about both themselves and the layout, varying their own behavior in attempts to perceive and use the environmental supports offered. A major shift in action patterns from crawling to walking upright is of prime interest as the environmental context presents surfaces with different affordances to be perceived, learned about, and acted on as an infant's powers of coping with locomotor problems are developing.

My third point concerns the contribution this research makes to the transfer of knowledge and skill. How specific is what is learned to both the situation presented and the action systems involved? This old question can be addressed anew because it has seldom, if ever, been asked about newly learned affordances. We assume that conceptual generalization eventually takes place, but the extent of generalization in the course of acquiring a major way of interacting with the world has seldom been the subject of study.

Back in the 1930s, when I was in graduate school, learning was the major topic of interest. The leading psychologists of the time (Hull and Tolman for me) thought, wrote, and argued about it. The chief question for many of us was transfer. Learning that was totally specific to a particular scene or occasion or muscle group would lead to inflexibility, not at all favorable for survival or evolution. Concepts like *stimulus generalization* were pushed as far as they could go as explanations, but they didn't go far enough. We worked hard on it, but the favored experimental paradigms were too narrow to serve well. *Learning set* represented a try at something broader, but the experiments were not realistic (apes or monkeys or retarded children repeatedly solved the same simple type of problem, such as the oddity problem, and achieved a degree of skill at just that problem). Eventually, the transfer question dropped out of fashion as cognitive psychology came in.

Understanding development of real, everyday behavior like navigating the environment fairly cries out for the study of transfer. This *Monograph* does more than merely revisit the problem. One method of locomotion, crawling, is learned and adapted successfully to navigation of potentially difficult or dangerous layouts, such as steep slopes. Well, wouldn't a means of coping with a potentially dangerous layout, such as a steep hill, be expected to generalize to a new method of locomotion, walking upright? Surprisingly, it does not. Walking is a whole new ball game. Babies who, as crawlers, learn to cope with a too-steep slope by sliding prone, or sitting, or some other safe means, will attempt too-steep slopes all over again when upright posture is first achieved.

But transfer does occur, as Adolph shows, in a much more subtle fashion. Learning is not specific to a particular layout or landscape or to a particular muscle group. Consider newly walking infants, faced with many different kinds of terrain—a drop-off at a bedside, a slippery floor, obstacles ahead, or a hill. Adolph shows, with appropriate control groups, that they do not learn to navigate each specific situation separately. The novice walkers do not learn that they cannot walk down those particular too-steep slopes, or exactly what angle constitutes too steep a slope, by practice on each one or by falling in that particular situation. As general walking skill develops, in their own homes and over whatever terrain they are normally exposed to, babies learn control of their own bodies and the limits of their physical abilities, at the same time attending to and differentiating the varied surfaces and layouts of the terrain that may occur. Detecting the subtle relation of these two is learning to perceive the affordances for mobility. It is a way of learning that makes flexibility of behavior attainable and guarantees greater modifiability and generality than the old notion of specific transfer from one problem to another of the same kind. The question becomes how flexibility of behavior is achieved rather than exactly what transfers. What is learned eventually is an ability to assess physical proficiency on-line, relative to the goal and to the environmental supports presently available.

In thinking about how affordances are learned, we need a new concept of transfer. Adolph's work suggests that acquiring a varied repertoire of means to an end and developing selectivity for adapting means to available contextual supports or lack of them are relevant to the question of transfer, rephrased as flexibility. Transfer is not accounted for by transfer of specialized acts, such as backing, from one situation (home) to another (the lab). It seems to be due to a much more general proficiency and control that enable flexible, adaptive behavior in the situations examined.

My fourth point is theoretical. The work described in this *Monograph* seems to me to be technically innovative and ingenious. New measures were needed for assessing development in the management of a locomotor problem, successful traversal of a slope. *Slope boundary* is a measure devised on the basis of traditional psychophysical methods, using a "staircasing" procedure. It captures the limit of slope safely manageable by an infant at a given moment in the developmental progression. This measure can then be used in relation to an infant's go ratio, an index that encapsulates the infant's performance at the relevant date with regard to the degree of slope actually attempted. It is possible, thus, to secure a measure of the adaptiveness of the individual's behavior and to observe the change in adaptiveness over time, especially as the method of locomotion shifts from crawling to walking.

A different, equally ingenious and useful procedure is the gait measure introduced for estimating development of walking skill. Inked felt pads on the baby's shoes leave a neat track of footprints on a roll of butcher paper. Appropriate measurements of angles of placement between the two feet and from one step to another yield sensitive measures of walking proficiency.

Locomotor development may not offer the ideal behavior for constructing a learning theory, but it certainly embodies some of the requirements. The task includes learning to detect information for guiding the route to a goal, for maintaining bodily balance during progression, and for estimating the safety of a given layout (flat stretch, hill, cliff, firm or compliant or slippery surface) for progression in one mode or another or not at all. Evolution has provided human infants with the ability to learn to do this as they grow in size, proficiency, and experience. Call it learning about affordances.

CONTRIBUTORS

Karen E. Adolph (Ph.D. 1993, Emory University) is an assistant professor of psychology at Carnegie Mellon University. Her research examines skill acquisition in infants, perceptual learning and the development of exploratory activity, and the development of posture and gait.

Bennett I. Bertenthal (Ph.D. 1978, University of Denver) is professor of psychology at the University of Virginia. He is currently on leave at the National Science Foundation, where he is the assistant director for social, behavioral, and economic sciences. His major research interests focus on the development of perception and action, the nonlinear modeling of developmental processes, and the perception of motion information.

Steven M. Boker (Ph.D. 1996, University of Virginia) is assistant professor of quantitative psychology at the University of Notre Dame. His methodological research interests include dynamic systems data analysis, structural equation modeling, and information theory. His substantive research interests include perception-action coupling and nonverbal communication analyzed from a dynamic systems perspective. He is a coauthor of the graphical user interface for the Mx Structural Equation Modeling software.

Eugene C. Goldfield (Ph.D. 1981, University of Connecticut) is research associate in psychiatry at Children's Hospital, Boston, and Harvard Medical School. His research focuses on the development of action in infants, with particular interest in the way that infants may explore their own actions to transform intrinsic dynamics into differentiated action systems. He is currently studying the effects of low birth weight on the coordination of oral and respiratory dynamics during the first two years.

Eleanor J. Gibson (Ph.D. 1938, Yale University) is the Susan Linn Sage Professor of Psychology Emerita at Cornell University. She is the author of *Principles of Perceptual Learning and Development* (1969), *The Psychology of Reading* (with Harry Levin, 1975), and *An Odyssey in Learning and Perception* (1991). She is a member of the National Academy of Sciences and a recipient of the National Medal of Science.

The *Monographs* series is intended as an outlet for major reports of developmental research that generate authoritative new findings and use these to foster a fresh and/or better-integrated perspective on some conceptually significant issue or controversy. Submissions from programmatic research projects are particularly welcome; these may consist of individually or group-authored reports of findings from some single large-scale investigation or of a sequence of experiments centering on some particular question. Multiauthored sets of independent studies that center on the same underlying question can also be appropriate; a critical requirement in such instances is that the various authors address common issues and that the contribution arising from the set as a whole be both unique and substantial. In essence, irrespective of how it may be framed, any work that contributes significant data and/or extends developmental thinking will be taken under editorial consideration.

Submissions should contain a minimum of 80 manuscript pages (including tables and references); the upper limit of 150–175 pages is much more flexible (please submit four copies; a copy of every submission and associated correspondence is deposited eventually in the archives of the SRCD). Neither membership in the Society for Research in Child Development nor affiliation with the academic discipline of psychology are relevant; the significance of the work in extending developmental theory and in contributing new empirical information is by far the most crucial consideration. Because the aim of the series is not only to advance knowledge on specialized topics but also to enhance cross-fertilization among disciplines or subfields, it is important that the links between the specific issues under study and larger questions relating to developmental processes emerge as clearly to the general reader as to specialists on the given topic.

Potential authors who may be unsure whether the manuscript they are planning would make an appropriate submission are invited to draft an outline of what they propose and send it to the Editor for assessment. This mechanism, as well as a more detailed description of all editorial policies, evaluation processes, and format requirements, is given in the "Guidelines for the Preparation of *Monographs* Submissions," which can be obtained by writing to the Editor, Rachel K. Clifton, Department of Psychology, University of Massachusetts, Amherst MA 01003.

DEMCO